COMPETING *with* CHARACTER℠

COMPETING *with* CHARACTER℠

Let's Put Sportsmanship and Fun Back in Youth Sports

Kevin Kush, M.A.,
with Michael Sterba, M.H.D.

BOYS TOWN℠
Press

Boys Town, Nebraska

COMPETING *with* CHARACTER

Published by the Boys Town Press
Father Flanagan's Boys' Home
Boys Town, Nebraska 68010

ISBN-13: 978-1-889322-98-8
ISBN-10: 1-889322-98-9

 **BOYS TOWN** ™
Saving Children   Healing Families

Boys Town Press is the publishing division of Boys Town, a national organization serving children and families.

Publisher's Cataloging in Publication Data

Kush, Kevin.

   Competing with character : let's put sportsmanship and fun back in youth sports / Kevin Kush ; with Michael Sterba. -- 1st ed. -- Boys Town, Neb. : Boys Town Press, c2008.

      p. ; cm.
      ISBN: 978-1-889322-98-8 ; 1-889322-98-9

      1. Sportsmanship--Study and teaching. 2. Coaching (Athletics)--Moral and ethical aspects. 3. Sports--Moral and ethical aspects. 4. Sports for children--Social aspects. I. Sterba, Michael. II. Title.

GV706.3 .K87 2008
796/.077--dc22   0808

10   9   8   7   6   5   4   3   2   1

Dedication

To every man or woman who answers to the name "Coach": By instilling character traits in young people today, you are helping create the leaders of tomorrow.

Acknowledgments

I would like to thank all of the Boys Town Press employees for their work on this project.

To my father Bernard, who died during the writing of this book, and to my mother Viola: Thank you for showing me what true character is!

To my wife Lynne and sons Keegan and Christian: Thanks for making me a better me.

To all of the Boys Town coaches: Thanks for making "work" such an enjoyable place.

And finally, thanks to Jesus Christ for helping me "Compete with Character" every day!

Boys Town would like to acknowledge Michael Josephson, president and founder of the Joseph & Edna Josephson Institute of Ethics, for his commitment and contributions to the development and advancement of character education for youth.

The partnership between the Josephson Institute and Boys Town on CHARACTER COUNTS! has led to seminal developments in Boys Town's character education programs, both in our schools and residential homes. We use CHARACTER COUNTS! with our kids every day. The concepts of CHARACTER COUNTS! influenced and inspired our Competing with Character program.

TABLE OF CONTENTS

What's Happening to Youth Sports?

PENNSYLVANIA – *During warm-ups before a youth T-ball game, a coach offers one of his players – an eight-year-old boy – twenty-five dollars to bean a teammate who is autistic and mildly retarded. The coach wants the autistic player injured so he can't play in the playoff game. When the first throw doesn't do the trick, the coach orders the eight-year-old to "hit him harder." So the young boy throws a second ball at his teammate's head, tearing his earlobe. A* *jury convicts the coach of criminal conspiracy to commit simple assault and corruption of minors.*

SOUTH DAKOTA – *At a youth soccer game, a coach strikes a referee, who is also the town's mayor. The match is between two eleven-year-old girls' teams. The coach is sentenced to forty-five days in jail, required to attend anger management classes, and banned from all youth sports for one year.*

NEVADA – *A parent of a twelve-year-old football player becomes angry when he learns that another player on the team is teasing his son. The parent seeks revenge on the player by trying to get him to drink from his son's water bottle that the parent has contaminated with an herbal extract that induces vomiting. Eight other players drink from the bottle and are poisoned. They are taken to area hospitals where they all recover. The parent is arrested and formally charged.*

MINNESOTA – *Two parents engage in a fight in front of forty children at a park. Hard feelings over playing time on a twelve-year-old girls' softball team erupts into a knock-down, drag-out fight between the two adults – with one accusing the other of biting off part of his earlobe. Charges are pending on both parents.*

CALIFORNIA – *A thirteen-year-old boy is charged with murder for a fatal attack on a fifteen-year-old boy who teased the younger child after a baseball game. The two boys had argued while waiting in line at the ballpark's snack bar. The younger boy grabbed his aluminum baseball bat and struck the older boy once in the leg, then delivered one deadly blow to his head.*

Out-of-control behavior on the fields and courts, along the sidelines, and in the stands is showing up more and more often in athletic competitions. This is troubling in and of itself, but what's most disturbing, as these stories demonstrate, is that it's happening among younger kids and in earlier levels of sports. Negative conduct from fans, coaches, and athletes has trickled down from professional sports to the college and high school ranks and is now infiltrating youth sports. Boys and girls as young as five and six years old are seeing coaches and parents lose control. Not only is this poor modeling of sportsmanship and fair play, but some of the behavior is also getting downright dangerous.

Not long ago, behavior such as a coach yelling at an official during a game, a parent in the stands complaining about his or her child's playing time, or a youngster "talking trash" to opposing players was considered obnoxious and unacceptable. Today, this kind of behavior is commonplace and accepted as the norm on many youth sports teams. Factors that have led to this current situation include an overemphasis on winning at all costs, early sports specialization, an increase in hyper-competitive or select teams and leagues, unrealistic hopes for sports scholarships to college, more parent misbehavior, and media emphasis on bad behavior by college and professional athletes, among others.

Some bad behavior has intensified and crossed over into thuggery and criminal actions. Too many adults and kids are brazenly escalating their words and actions beyond what should be acceptable at youth athletic contests. It's alarming and disturbing to see coaches, parents, and youngsters arrested and hauled off to jail over a *kids'*

3

game that sometimes involves participants as young as five, six, and seven!

The earlier stories paint a bleak picture of the current state of youth sports, and they make it hard to deny that something is broken and in need of repair. These incidents also can be seen as cries for help, indicators that we've veered off course. When the adults who are involved and in charge of youth sports lose perspective and even self-control, we have a major problem.

We are at a pivotal time in organized youth sports. It's not too late to get kids playing the games for the right reasons – so they can learn good sportsmanship and good character, and just have fun. We must sound a rallying cry to all those involved, especially coaches and parents. Now is the time to take a collective breath, look at where we are and how we got here, and decide where we want to go.

In 2005, the Citizenship Through Sports Alliance (CTSA) released a national report card (see page 5) that provided a disturbing assessment of today's youth sporting environment. The largest coalition of professional and amateur athletic organizations in the United States (see the bottom of the report card for a complete list of CTSA members), the CTSA asked a panel of youth sports experts from across the country to evaluate youth sports in the United States and report on its successes and failures in areas including coaching, officiating, and parental behavior. In almost every major category reviewed, the Alliance gave barely passing grades. Of great concern was that the worst grades were given in the areas of putting children first and the behaviors of parents. (For more details about each category and to view the complete CTSA "2005 Youth Sports National Report Card," see Appendix 1.)

2005 CSTA Youth Sports National Report Card

AREA OF REVIEW	GRADE
Child-Centered Philosophy	D
Coaching	C-
Health and Safety	C+
Officiating	B-
Parental Behavior/Involvement	D

CTSA Members include: National Collegiate Athletic Association (NCAA); Major League Baseball (MLB); National Basketball Association (NBA) and Women's National Basketball Association (WNBA); National Hockey League (NHL); National Federation of State High School Associations (NFHS); National Association of Intercollegiate Athletics (NAIA); National Association for Sport and Physical Education (NASPE); National Junior College Athletic Association (NJCAA); and National Association of Collegiate Directors of Athletics (NACDA).

Reports like this reveal the fundamental problems that exist in youth sports today. Now that the problems are out in the open for all to see, it's time to fix what's broken in youth sports.

Into Action!

While bad behavior usually gets the media head-lines, it's not all doom and gloom out there in youth sports land. Far from it! Take coach Jim Johnson and student Jason McElwain of Greece Athena High School near Rochester, New York. Jason has autism. Although he didn't make the high school's basketball team, he had such passion for the game that he stayed on as team manager. Coach Johnson was impressed with Jason's dedication throughout the year. To reward him, the coach added Jason to the roster for the season's final home game and let him suit up and sit on the bench. With four minutes remaining, Johnson put Jason in the game. In those last four minutes, Jason scored twenty points! Everyone in attendance went wild with each basket. The celebration peaked when Jason hit his sixth three-point basket at the buzzer. In the gym that day, no one lost. Players, coaches, parents, and spectators for both teams were treated to a special sports moment because the coach realized how important it was for Jason to be part of the game and team he loved. The highlights of the game were replayed repeatedly on ESPN and many other major media outlets carried the inspiring story.

All across America, every day, there are kids and adults having good experiences in youth sports. Most of these happen without publicity or fanfare but they're still dramatic, important, and spectacular to the children, coaches, parents, and fans who are there. There's the twelve-year-old volleyball player who finally gets her first overhand serve over the net for a point, or the eight-year-old boy who scores his first soccer goal, or the ten-year-old baseball player who catches a pop fly for the final out of an inning. Girls and boys who participate in youth sports just want and need the opportunity to play, have fun, and work toward success.

Most adults who are involved in youth sports are good people trying to do the right things for kids. They have a strong desire to help youngsters grow and learn through participation in organized sports. The problem is that a few bad eggs can do a lot of harm to a lot of young people very quickly. And the number of bad eggs seems to be growing.

One problem is that many well-intentioned adults simply lack the training and expertise to know how to create an athletic environment for girls and boys that's positive, fun, safe, and caring, as well as successful. Many youth sports coaches are simply parents who volunteer to do the job. It's easy for enthusiastic, but untrained coaches to become focused on winning to the exclusion of other goals that should be important in youth sports. It's tough to stay committed to making sure kids are having fun, learning athletic skills, and playing with character when others are looking only at your won-loss record. Education and training, however, can help coaches, parents, and players stay on track to make the youth sports scene both enjoyable and successful.

This book is about solutions and taking action. *Competing with Character* is an innovative and exciting approach to teaching kids how to participate in sports with sportsmanship and character. The program grew out of the Teaching Model employed at Boys Town, a national organization serving youth and families. The Model emphasizes the importance of teaching not only at-risk and troubled youngsters, but all children, how to use new skills, how to build positive and healthy relationships, and how to go about making good choices. This approach works! We've seen the miracle of change at

Boys Town in thousands of girls and boys who've gone out into the world and succeeded.

The main goal of the *Competing with Character* program is for youngsters, parents, and coaches to learn and use new skills. Each group has different roles and responsibilities in youth sports, so there are three sets of skills, one each specially designed for coaches, parents, and participants. There are eight skills for coaches, seven for parents, and ten for players. Coaching skills, for example, include how to correct kids' misbehavior and how to communicate with parents. Parents should compliment rather then criticize their young athletes and model appropriate behavior at games. Children need to be taught to listen to their coaches and respect their opponents, among other skills. In addition, there are three teaching methods coaches and parents can use to help kids learn their skills. When all the skills are working together and being used correctly, they help create an environment where adults and kids promote and practice good sportsmanship and character. In addition, the skills help everyone keep the youth sports experience in the proper perspective: The games are for kids to enjoy and learn from and not for adults to exploit.

Years of research at Boys Town have shown that skill teaching can lead to better behavior and performance in many areas of a person's life. *Competing with Character* offers many skills that work as well in the outside world as they do in the world of youth sports. Skills like "Following Instructions" and "Voicing Concerns Appropriately" can help young people and adults in their interactions not only in athletics but also at school and on the job.

What are the benefits of incorporating and using skills like these in your sports setting? When kids learn how to follow instructions, coaches are better able to have practices that are organized, productive, and fun for both kids and coaches. And, when parents and coaches learn how to voice concerns appropriately, it leads to better communication. This can result in a more enjoyable, upbeat, and supportive experience and relationship between all the adults. The skills that make up the *Competing with Character* program give you new ways to think and act that can improve on and enhance what you're already doing with kids. What you're really getting are some new tools for your youth sports toolbox.

Whether you run a league or a club filled with many teams, coach a single team, or are a parent who wants his or her child to have a healthy and positive experience in organized sports, you can benefit from what's in these pages. I offer you the opportunity to become a member of a larger team that understands the importance of and knows how to compete with character. I challenge you to take action and become part of the solution!

A Lifetime of Sports

Athletics has played a major role in my life and helped shape the person I am today. I spent much of my

---

In addition to this book, Boys Town has developed a training workshop for schools, clubs, leagues, and teams to formally introduce their coaches and parents to the *Competing with Character* program and its goals, expectations, skills, and teaching methods. There is a training session for coaches and one for parents. To learn more about this energizing workshop, please visit the following Web site: www.boystown.org.

---

childhood and teen years playing sports, both unstruc-tured games on the playgrounds, courts, and fields in my neighborhood and supervised competitions on orga-nized teams and leagues. My youth sports experience was a positive one, and I continued to participate in athletics all the way through high school. Ultimately, I earned an athletic scholarship to play football in college at the University of Nebraska at Omaha. While there, I realized my calling was to help young people through teaching and coaching.

Over the last two decades, I've been a high school football coach and teacher. I spent my first nine years as a football coach and business education teacher at a large public high school in Omaha, Nebraska. During my time there, we won many games, including a state champion-ship; we were runner-up another year. We were a peren-nial powerhouse in the largest and most talented high school football league in the state.

In 1996, an unexpected phone call came my way. The superintendent of Boys Town High School said that some other coaches had recommended me as a person who would be a good fit for the vacant head coaching position at Boys Town High School. I was hesitant about interviewing for the job because I knew little about Boys Town and what went on there. But, after visiting the cam-pus and meeting some kids, my decision and path were clear. I wanted to be part of the Boys Town mission of sav-ing children and healing families.

The centerpiece of Boys Town's work with kids is its residential treatment program located on its Home Campus in the Village of Boys Town, Nebraska. Kids who come here are often unmotivated and usually academi-cally, behaviorally, and/or emotionally challenged. At Boys Town, boys and girls live separately in homes in a family-style environment where married couples provide the warmth, structure, and treatment necessary to allow healing to take place. The campus includes a high school and middle school, both with full athletic and academic programs. While some youth live at Boys Town for many years and graduate from high school here, the average length of stay for a boy or girl is about eighteen months. This creates a unique challenge when trying to build a successful sports program year in and year out.

Boys Town's football team, the Cowboys, play in a much smaller league than my previous team did. Also, the talent level in the league and on the Cowboys' team is much lower than what I was accustomed to. Most Boys Town players have never played organized football before. We even have to teach players how to put on their pads and uniforms correctly! Many days, I don't know who'll be at practice because if a youngster misbehaves badly enough at school or in the home, he won't be playing football that day.

We had a rough season my first year as head football coach, winning only one game. The second year, we finished the season with eight wins and three losses and made the state playoffs. The following year, we went all the way to the state semi-finals. Over the past eleven years, we've made the state playoffs every year and have been a fixture in the state's Top Ten ratings. In 2005, we won eleven games and again made it to the state semi-finals. And in 2007, we had another successful season and reached the second round of the state playoffs.

At Boys Town High School, our athletic programs and sports teams are important because they help instill a sense of community and pride in troubled boys and girls, most of whom have never experienced these things before. On an individual level, participation in sports is therapeutic; it's another way to help youngsters heal. My experience here has allowed me to see the real value of athletics and to keep it all in the proper perspective. Youth sports should be only a part of the fabric that makes up a young person's life, not the whole foundation.

In addition to what I've seen and experienced in athletics both personally and professionally, I'm the parent of two boys, Keegan and Christian. Both participate in youth sports. Needless to say, over the years, I've seen the good, the bad, and the ugly in the conduct of players, parents, fans, and coaches. I've also got a lot invested here! I believe in the power of athletics and the positive, supportive role they can play in helping to shape loving, caring, and productive people. *Competing with Character* was developed so we can share with you and other adults involved in youth sports how to create a healthy and positive environment where girls and boys can have fun, learn, and grow in youth sports.

Athletic competition has been an influential and constructive part of the lives of countless young people for many, many years. That can continue, but there are some things that need to be fixed and cleaned up for it to really be effective. It's up to us – the coaches and parents – to be courageous and say enough already! It's time we band together and make the changes necessary to bring youth sports back into the proper perspective so young people can benefit from all that athletics has to offer.

Making This Book Part of Your Lineup

Competing with Character is a proven method that's easy to understand and implement. You're given specific skills that demonstrate good character and sportsmanship and particular ways to teach them. These tools allow you to easily integrate the *Competing with Character* program into any youth sports setting. The program enhances all the good things you're already doing, while giving young athletes, their parents, and coaches new ways of thinking and behaving that promote and build a positive and fun atmosphere.

The next chapter in this book assesses the current state of youth sports, its problems, and what youth sports should look like. It begins to focus on solutions and how the *Competing with Character* program can provide you with the necessary answers. Chapter 3 discusses the role of social skills for kids in promoting character in youth sports, and how to teach them to children. The next three chapters address the core of the *Competing with Character* program. We'll first address coaches and parents because kids' learning starts with us – how we act as teachers and role models. There is a chapter for coaches and a chapter for parents, both of which provide specific skills, or things to do and ways to act, that teach and model good character and sportsmanship. The last chapter is devoted to skills for players.

Changing the focus and culture of your team's or organization's players, parents, and coaches might seem like a difficult task. However, I firmly believe that once everyone involved understands the gravity of the situation and how easily it can be remedied, they'll enthusiastically jump on board! Youth sports are too fertile a training ground for lessons that last a lifetime to surrender it to an obsession with wins and losses, unrealistic hopes about college scholarships, and other grandiose and outrageous expectations.

❮❮ *It has always been a source of* great
satisfaction to me to watch
a child acquire strength and
dignity of character. Children acquire
character through their desire to emulate and
practice the principles of right living laid before
them by those they love and respect. ❯❯

— FATHER EDWARD FLANAGAN
FOUNDER OF BOYS TOWN

14

IT'S ONLY A GAME

Youth sports began in a relaxed, carefree environment where girls and boys competed for fun in their free time. They would gather at local parks, dusty sandlots, and driveway basketball courts after school and on the weekends to play games with neighborhood friends. The kids were in charge and made all the decisions about issues like team captains, who was on each team, and the rules of the game.

Adults were nowhere in sight and rarely became involved, unless there was major trouble. Most of the time when kids disagreed about something, they managed to work things out just fine by themselves. Perhaps most importantly, young people seemed to keep sports in the right perspective. They played to have fun, be with friends, keep fit, and participate with others.

It's fun to reminisce about the "good old days." But we all know that change is an inevitable part of life, and youth sports are no exception. The days of youngsters being in charge and figuring things out for themselves are a thing of the past. Unstructured games not monitored by adults are now more the exception than the rule. Today, youth sports are organized, run, and controlled by adults. They direct and guide girls and boys through every move, govern all aspects of the youth sports setting, and make decisions that young people used to make and learn from themselves.

This change started slowly but has really picked up steam over the last few decades. Today, adult influence on youth sports is stronger than ever. Several societal trends have helped shape this movement.

First, sports have exploded as a central form of entertainment and a major leisure time activity for adults and kids. The media – especially television and the Internet and their twenty-four/seven "all access, all the time" coverage – have helped fuel a national obsession with sports, sporting events, and athletes. This fascination is no longer confined only to the professional level; it's trickled down to the college and high school scenes – and more recently, it's invaded youth sports. In the lives of many people and families, athletics have become so consuming that other important aspects of life like academics, the arts, and family time have been pushed into the background.

Another trend is our society's emphasis on competition in almost every aspect of life. Many people compete with others over who has the best job, nicest house, most money, greenest lawn, etc. This attitude is nothing new, but what is new is that it's spread to youth sports and their participants. Parents compete with each other over whose ten-year-old is the best player or who's the real star on the high school varsity squad or who's being recruited for a college scholarship. There's a certain status – a badge of honor of sorts – attached to these youngsters and their families. Today in youth sports, many adults, families, and kids are working hard (and spending hard-earned money) not just to keep up with the Joneses but to blow right by them in athletic competition!

A final reason adults have become so involved in youth sports is more practical: Our neighborhoods and playgrounds aren't as safe as they once were. In many places, there's a disconnect between neighborhoods and neighbors. The old mindset of "you watch and discipline my kids and I'll do the same with yours" has faded as neighbors have grown further apart and become more isolated. So, parents don't feel comfortable allowing their children to wander unsupervised too far from the safety of home. Some parents won't let their children play tag with friends on the front lawn, let alone run down to the local park to get in on a pick-up game.

Whatever the reasons, is it necessarily a bad thing that adults have taken control of youth sports? The best answer is that there are always positives and negatives that come with change. One positive result of the governing presence of adults in youth sports is the dramatic rise in the number of organized youth sports teams and leagues. For example, in 2006, U.S. Soccer reported that youth soccer numbers rose from about fifteen million participants in 1987 to more than seventeen and a half million in 2002 (the latest year for which numbers are available). Also, Pop Warner Football reported that participation nearly doubled in the last fifteen years, from about 130,000 players to 260,000 players. Girls and boys of all ages have more opportunities than ever before to get involved in almost any sport at nearly any level of development, commitment, and competition.

On the other hand, one of the biggest problems of this relatively new phenomenon in youth sports lies with the very fact that adults are running the show. What kids used to figure out and learn through trial and error is now provided for them. The secondary learning that used to take place during unstructured and unsupervised play has been replaced by an organized plan that kids follow without having any say in what happens. Everything is neatly laid out by adults for youth to obey and follow – when to practice and play, who is on what team, what rules are used, how much everyone will play, and more.

Other problems have arisen from the way today's youth sports are organized and run. Many adults have a win-at-all-cost mentality that promotes hyper-competition, even among the youngest age groups. And kids are specializing in one sport while excluding all others at earlier and earlier ages. They play that sport year round for select and club teams that require expensive fees for participation and travel. Playing a single sport exclusively, however, can lead to burnout and overuse injuries.

Other problems involve coach, parent, and spectator misbehavior. Much of it results from adults replacing the child-centered goals and perspectives (participate and have fun) in youth sports with adult-centered goals and perspectives (winning is the only thing). This leads to over-invested adults who have unrealistic expectations for young athletes, display poor behavior at youth games, and fail to consider appropriate developmental goals for children.

Media and society tend to over-emphasize the importance of sports. Dazzled by all the celebrity-type attention devoted to professional athletes, many young people put sports stars – some of whom have sordid pasts and troubled lives – on a pedestal as role models. The media often focus on drug and steroid use, and other negative sports stories that promote the wrong ideals and values to kids.

It's important for coaches, parents, and fans like you to be aware of these problems and the potential for them to occur. Equally important is always keeping the youth sports experience in proper focus – that it exists for the benefit and enjoyment of the child. Keeping these two factors in mind can head off potential negative outcomes and steer your youth sports programs down a positive path. That's where our *Competing with Character* program comes in. When properly implemented and followed, the program can help ensure that your youth sports environment is as healthy, productive, and positive a place as possible for youngsters to learn and grow.

It Just Doesn't Add Up

One issue that constantly clouds youth sports is the unrealistic expectation many adults have that a young girl or boy will be able to star in high school sports and ultimately earn a scholarship to play in college. Too many parents also believe their child has a good chance to become a professional athlete as well. Unfortunately, the facts say otherwise.

The National Council of Youth Sports has reported that more than forty-one million girls and boys currently participate in some kind of organized youth sport annually (school-sponsored, YMCA, select or club team, etc.). Experts estimate, however, that more than seventy percent of children quit organized youth sports by age thirteen, or before they enter high school. Youngsters report these reasons as why they stopped playing organized sports:

- *"I'm not interested anymore."*
- *"It's not fun anymore."*
- *"The coach played favorites/was a poor teacher/was too negative."*
- *"It took up too much time."*
- *"I want to get involved and participate in other activities."*
- *"There was too much pressure."*

What about the kids who do keep playing sports after junior high school? The NCAA currently reports that nearly seven million girls and boys play sports in high school. Of these nearly seven million participants, only about 126,000 student-athletes will receive either a partial or full athletic scholarship to play sports in college. That means less than two percent of all high school athletes will have the opportunity to translate their athletic success into financial assistance for college. And the chances of having a professional sports career are even slimmer: The odds of a high school athlete becoming a pro player is one in 1,250 for football, one in 3,300 for men's basketball, and one in 5,000 for women's basketball.

Even though these facts might be hard to accept, there's a high likelihood that your child will stop playing sports before he or she even enters high school. If your child does participate in high school sports, it's highly unlikely that he or she will play college sports, let alone earn an athletic scholarship. And it takes a "perfect storm" – the right combination of a lot of talent, hard work, and luck – for a youngster to go on to play sports professionally.

These statistics are especially startling and sobering to many adults who are heavily involved in organized youth sports. Most of those coaches and parents just assume young people will continue playing organized sports in high school, maybe in college, and possibly even professionally. The cold, hard truth is that the vast majority of girls and boys decide to hang up the uniform before they leave junior high school.

So why should kids stay in organized youth sports? The best answer is that young people can come away with something that helps them grow and mature – if the activity they participate in is done right. The greatest gifts kids can receive from their youth sports experience are new skills and lessons they can take with them and apply to other areas of their lives. Sure, we want youngsters to become better athletes. But in the end, it's most important that they walk away from their sports experience as better people. That's why adults must focus their teaching on good character and sportsmanship, while creating an environment that promotes the child-centered goals of fun, friends, fitness, and participation.

This is why our *Competing with Character* program was specifically developed for youth sports age groups. The window of opportunity to teach youngsters character skills and lessons though participation in sports is open only for a short time. So it's imperative to make good use of the time we have with kids by taking advantage of the fertile teaching opportunities youth athletics have to offer.

What Kids Are Saying about Youth Sports

The tremendous growth of organized youth sports has led to many positive outcomes for kids. Youngsters really learn and grow from their youth sports experience when adults focus their time, energy, and teaching on creating an atmosphere that supports and enhances what the kids want and need. At first glance, this might seem hard to do because young people participate in sports for so many different reasons. However, surveys by experts echo common themes for why youngsters say they want to play organized sports. The top reasons include:

- *"I want to have fun."*
- *"I want to do something I'm good at."*
- *"I want to be with friends and make new ones."*
- *"I want to get fit and stay in shape."*
- *"I want to learn new skills and improve on existing ones."*
- *"I want to play and participate as a member of a team."*

These all come from the child's point of view and tell adults exactly what kids want to get out of their athletic experience. These are the reasons coaches and parents should be paying attention to and using as the foundation of their youth sports setting. We shouldn't be surprised to see that "having fun" tops the list. That's easy to understand. After all, why would anyone (youth or adult) want to engage in a hobby or extracurricular activity they don't enjoy? "Having fun" should be at the top of your list too, and be a focal point of your athletic environment.

Many adults are surprised to see that young people consistently rank "winning" toward the bottom on surveys about why they play sports. Many adults in today's society stress and value winning and being number one – it's that competition fixation. But the vast majority of kids don't care all that much about wins and losses (at least not until adults have convinced them that it's all-important). Children value fun, friends, fitness, learning new skills, and participation more.

Now, I'm not suggesting athletes and their coaches shouldn't be competitive, strive for excellence, and work diligently to win. Winning should be one of the goals any time a team or individual competes. Wins and losses, however, shouldn't be the sole measuring stick for success, especially with young girls and boys involved in youth sports. Knowing how to demonstrate good character and show positive sportsmanship skills after a disheartening loss can be a much more valuable and long-lasting life lesson than the fleeting good feelings that come from a victory.

The question coaches and parents should ask themselves is this: Am I doing everything possible to help kids meet their goals? Unfortunately, for too many adults involved in youth sports, the honest answer is "No." They are not putting young people's aspirations ahead of their own. They are not in tune with what kids truly want to take away from their athletic experience. They have not adjusted their priorities to match those of the kids. They have not created an environment where kids' interests and objectives come first.

Competing with Character can help reverse this trend. Here's what can happen when adults organize and run youth sports to do what's best for their young athletes:

- Kids are among friends and develop a sense of belonging.

- Youth learn new physical and behavioral skills.

- Youngsters learn character and sportsmanship skills and lessons that can be used in other areas of life.

- Kids are able to engage in regular physical activity that can lead to better overall fitness and help them lead healthier lives.

- Kids improve their self-confidence and sense of self-worth, helping them gain maturity.

- Girls and boys can become more socially competent, which includes developing positive interpersonal skills.

- Participation in sports tends to lead to higher test results in school.

- Participation in sports promotes moral development.

While all these are valuable to helping young people learn and grow through sports, let's focus on the last benefit on the list – moral development.

In 2004, The Institute for the Study of Youth Sports at Michigan State University conducted a research project for the Citizenship Through Sports Alliance organization. In this study, the Institute reported that research on "…the benefits of moral development has been the most debated. Researchers have questioned the notion that 'sports builds character' as an automatic by-product of sports participation (Coakley, 2004; Weiss & Smith, 2002). Rather, character must be specifically 'taught' versus 'caught' (Hodge, 1989). Moreover, research has demonstrated that when fair play, sportsmanship, and moral development information is systematically and consistently taught to children in sport and physical education settings, character can be enhanced (Bredemeier, Weiss, Shield, & Shewchuk, 1986; Gibbins, Ebbeck, & Weiss, 1995)."

The information gleaned from this research is valuable and important to the youth sports world. The experts are telling us that kids don't automatically learn and develop character and sportsmanship skills just because they play sports. These skills aren't just "caught"; they must be taught. And they need to be taught with an approach that's organized, structured, and dependable.

What this means for you is that you can't just make it up on the fly. You need a program like *Competing with Character* to provide you with a specific plan for promoting good character and sportsmanship, and proven methods to teach them. With this approach, there's no guessing or hoping.

What *Competing with Character* Brings to Your Lineup

The youth sports experience can bring so much to kids' lives. It's imperative that coaches and parents create and maintain the right atmosphere, one where their goals and perspectives are set aside in favor of those of the children's. When you do this, you've taken the first step toward creating the ultimate athletic environment. But there is more to it. You can create many positive outcomes when you strive toward excellence in your youth sports setting.

The ideal sports setting:

- Creates a culture where good character is a priority.

- Is a place where practices and games are enjoyable and fun for kids and for adults.

- Increases outward displays of sportsmanship and positive behavior by coaches, parents, athletes, and spectators that are the norm rather than the exception.

- Teaches girls and boys valuable life skills.

- Reduces coach frustration both during practices and games.

- Creates a more positive, helpful, and open relationship between coaches and parents.

- Increases communication between coaches, athletes, and parents.

- Reduces poor sportsmanship and bad behavior by adults and kids.

- Is viewed by others as a positive and healthy place for kids.

Who wouldn't want all these benefits for their kids, coaches, parents, and spectators? *Competing with Character* helps you bring all these and more to your athletic environment. The program enables coaches and parents to put kids first and create an approach to a sports team, league, or club that's right on target. It allows you to be the best in every way.

We must find a way to turn the corner in our attitude toward sports in general and youth sports in particular, one coach, one parent, one organization at a time. No matter what level of competition your youngsters are at – select or travel, recreational or club, Y League or church league, jayvee or varsity – teaching the principles of character and good sportsmanship should lead off your lineup! In the next chapter, we'll show you how to begin doing this.

" *Character is formed by doing the thing we are supposed to do, when it should be done, whether we feel like doing it or not.* **"**

– FATHER EDWARD FLANAGAN

CHAPTER

READY...SET...TEACH!

Kids aren't born knowing how to tie their shoes or feed themselves. As toddlers, they don't know how to make a bed, do the dishes, or use the toilet. Even when they start school, some children aren't yet able to print their ABC's or count to twenty without using their fingers and toes.

Children have to *learn* the skills they're going to need to use as they grow up. Skills are not magically absorbed as kids get older, and learning is not a one-time thing where you teach a skill once and a child is good to go. As adults, we have to teach these skills over and over, making sure that a child is both old enough and developmentally ready to learn them. And teaching involves more than just telling a child what to do – it also means demonstrating, modeling, and practicing the skills until he or she knows how, when, where, and why to use them.

Many times, we assume kids know how to behave correctly and understand how to make choices that are best for themselves and others. However, girls and boys need direction and guidance in almost every area of their lives. It might be something as simple as showing them how to clean their bedroom or something more complicated like how to accept defeat graciously. Whatever the circumstances, learning involves behaviors, skills, and teaching.

Coaches, parents, and other adults who spend time with kids do lots of great teaching every day. At Boys Town, we've spent more than ninety years developing the best ways to help kids learn, grow, and, succeed. Decades of research show that our skill-based, teaching approach is a highly effective and successful method, whether you're working with kids as a parent or as a youth sports coach.

In this chapter, we'll define what behaviors and skills are and discuss why they are important to your teaching with kids. Also, we'll introduce three methods you can use to teach behaviors and skills to youngsters. Finally, we'll talk about giving "reasons" and their importance to children in learning and using skills.

Competing with Character's skill-based, teaching approach helps everyone – coaches, athletes, and parents – set and achieve positive goals in the sports arena and in other settings like home and school. Teaching behaviors and skills to kids, and having coaches and parents adapt and model new ones for how they participate, is the foundation for creating an atmosphere of good character, sportsmanship, and success. Learning skills and knowing how to use them helps kids and adults solve problems, resolve conflicts, and respond to situations with behaviors that are positive and constructive, rather than negative and destructive.

What You Don't Know *Can* Hurt You

Often, youngsters (and some adults) don't use the right behaviors or interact with others in a positive way simply because they don't know what they're supposed to do in certain situations. For example, when young kids lose a close, exciting game for the first time, they're likely to be upset or angry and prone to react in inappropriate ways. They might throw their equipment around, refuse to congratulate or shake hands with the other team, or blame the officials. Instead, we can prepare them to handle adversity by teaching them the right ways to behave toward their teammates, coaches, and opponents in such a situation. It's up to adults to teach kids the behaviors and skills they need to function and find success.

We define a behavior as anything a person does or says that can be directly or indirectly observed (seen, heard, felt, touched, or smelled) and measured. Skills are sets of behaviors that usually are done in a particular order to achieve a goal or accomplish a task. For example, the skill of "Following Instructions" includes these individual behaviors: look at the person, say "Okay," do what you've been asked to do right away, and check back when the task is completed. When kids learn and use this skill, they're

31

more likely to be successful in many different settings (sports, school, home, etc.) and situations. It's also a skill that helps adults create organized, smooth-running learning environments where kids do what's asked of them.

Coaches teach athletic behaviors and skills all the time. Most involve physical skills, like how to shoot a basketball, where you explain, demonstrate, and practice a series of physical behaviors kids need to master to be successful. For example, when teaching a player how to shoot a basketball, you might go over hand and finger position, how to use the legs, elbow position, and follow through. To make your teaching most effective, you would have the player practice each component (or behavior) until it's mastered. Then you would work on helping the youngster put all the components together to perform the skill of shooting a basketball.

Teaching character and sportsmanship skills follows the same pattern – introduce each of the behaviors that make up the skill, put all the behaviors together, and have youngsters practice them until they've mastered the skill.

Skills Help Kids Succeed

Teaching, learning, and using character and sportsmanship skills have many benefits for coaches, parents, and kids. The relatively short time you spend on this kind of teaching during practices and games will ultimately pay off in a better learning environment and will give you more time to coach and teach. When girls and boys are able to use the skills we recommend, a coach's job becomes easier because players are listening, following instructions, using positive behaviors and skills, and making decisions that allow the team to work together and move forward.

Here's an example: Let's say you're coaching a baseball team or basketball team of eight-year-olds. If you can help them learn how to pay attention to you and the other coaches and follow instructions, you can eliminate many of the problems you might run into during practices and games. When kids know how to do these two things consistently, you won't have to repeat yourself a dozen times or always check to make sure the players are doing what you ask.

Teaching skills that focus on the basics and contribute to character building creates an atmosphere where there are fewer conflicts, more cooperation, better communication, and a greater sense of pride in a team's and organization's reputation for sportsmanship. Visible, frequent signs of good sportsmanship reflect this positive attitude. And who wouldn't want to be a part of that?

It's also important for adults to use and demonstrate good character skills in a youth sports setting. Kids learn most of what they say and do from watching the adults around them. When coaches and parents use sportsmanship skills, they model positive behavior for youngsters and show them that sportsmanship and character are important qualities for the team and organization. Modeling positive character behaviors and skills is the best way for you to be part of the solution!

In the next three chapters, we're going to review a number of skills for coaches and parents that help promote and model good sportsmanship, better communication, and respect for everyone involved – teammates, officials, opponents, and fans. We'll also present a number of skills that coaches can teach their players and parents can reinforce at home. These skills not only help girls and boys learn sportsmanship and character on the field or court, but also help them find success at home, in school, and in many other social situations. Before we move on, though, let's go over the methods you can use to teach these skills.

Teaching

How you teach skills to young people is often as important as what you're teaching. Coaches and parents must have effective methods and a planned approach for helping kids learn new skills, improve on existing ones, and get better at choosing the right skills to use in specific situations. This is true whether you're instructing kids on how to serve a volleyball or how to get along with their teammates.

The teaching methods covered in this section come from the Boys Town Teaching Model. They're proven techniques designed to make skill teaching successful. These three approaches – teaching proactively, using praise, and correcting misbehavior – work together to help you prevent problem behavior, reinforce good behavior, and correct inappropriate behavior.

Prepare and Practice

Proactive Teaching is a way for coaches and parents to introduce new skills and help kids practice them before kids need to use them. This teaching method mirrors how coaches prepare their players for an upcoming game. Good coaches spend a lot of time setting up their team and players for success by teaching fundamental skills and developing a plan to use them in a game, practicing them over and over until they've been mastered, and then quickly reviewing the game plan just before the team hits the field or court.

You can use this proactive approach with any skill, including those that promote character and sportsmanship. For example, before a game you might remind players to not trash-talk or make rude gestures, to play within the rules, and to ignore any unsportsmanlike behavior from their opponents. Or, before you begin practice you might spend a few minutes telling your players that when a coach is talking, they should stop what they are doing, look at the coach, and make an effort to concentrate on what he or she is saying.

To set kids up for success in many different situations, it is important that you spend small amounts of time beforehand teaching new skills and reviewing behaviors and skills you've already taught. Just like a winning game plan, proper preparation and good execution are the keys to successfully teaching character skills!

Praise Works Wonders!

Everyone likes praise. It's a motivator that lets a person know he or she did something well and that someone noticed. A pat on the back or a word of congratulations makes us feel good, both about what we've done and who we are. This is especially true for children and teens. They love it when adults who are important in their lives notice they've used or tried to use a positive behavior.

Our motto at Boys Town is "Catch 'em being good!" For many adults, this kind of approach doesn't come naturally and is sometimes difficult to adopt. Why? Because many people simply expect kids to use the correct behavior or skill, do the right thing, and make good choices. They believe youngsters should be doing these things anyway, so why praise them? However, many girls and boys struggle to use the correct behavior or skill at the right time, do the right thing, and make sound decisions.

Another reason praise is sometimes underused is that it's easy to focus on "bad" behavior or mistakes. Misbehavior is more obvious and "in your face." So we tend to notice and react to the bad behaviors and either ignore or forget to let youngsters know when they've done well.

Good coaches and parents rely heavily on giving praise, positive reinforcement, and positive consequences. At Boys Town, we focus on what our girls and boys do right and use lots of praise with them. We certainly correct youth for inappropriate behavior, but we also look for many more opportunities to praise and reinforce youngsters for using positive behavior. With some kids, we might use a very high rate of praise; it all depends on the youth and his or her individual needs (we'll discuss this more later in the book).

Praising and reinforcing young people when they do something right motivates them to repeat positive behaviors and skills and lets them know you see their good behavior as well as their bad behavior. For example, you might teach kids the skill of listening to adults. Then, when you're explaining something to youngsters and see them stop what they are doing, look at you, and concentrate on what you say, praise them! Give them a pat on the back and tell them exactly what they did right so they can do it again. Praise, reinforcement, and positive consequences help young people feel confident about themselves and their ability to succeed.

Right the Wrong

No one does everything perfectly all the time, especially kids who are learning new behaviors and skills.

They will get frustrated and upset sometimes as they try to master what you're teaching. So you can expect some bumps along the way.

While it's important to praise youngsters for using appropriate behaviors and skills whenever possible and to prepare them for situations where they will have to use certain skills, there will be times when you have to correct a child's misbehavior. This is when teaching is the most important. You have to step up and teach them the right behaviors and skills. If you don't, they'll continue to misbehave and fail.

When you're the adult in charge, you control the setting and how it runs. You do not control the kids. Why? Because they have to make choices for themselves. However, you can influence those choices. One of the most important ways you do this is through teaching and giving consequences. Praise and reward good choices, but don't hesitate to correct poor ones. For example, if you expect your players to remain quiet while a coach is talking (and you've taught this skill), and you observe two players constantly giggling and whispering back and forth, call them on it. Address the inappropriate behavior, correct it by teaching them the right behavior, and (if needed) give them a negative consequence. When the players are quiet and paying attention to you, praise them and reinforce the positive behavior.

A word of caution about negative consequences: They are not supposed to be punishing or a way to "get back" at a child who misbehaves. Rather, they should be deterrents to future misbehavior and motivators for good behavior. Consistently using appropriate consequences helps change behavior. Also, make sure the negative consequences you use are appropriate for the age and developmental level of the kids you're working with. For example, it's inappropriate to make a ten-year-old do a hundred pushups or run sprints the last thirty minutes of practice. It might be more appropriate and effective to have that child sit out for ten minutes on the bench or jog a lap around the field. Negative consequences can be difficult to choose if you don't know what motivates each child. Get to know your youngsters and what they either enjoy or dislike so you can choose positive and negative consequences that will change their behavior.

It's Okay to Explain Why

Parents and coaches are notorious for using the reason, *"Because I said so. That's why!"*, when a child questions their instructions or decisions. We've learned that it's much more effective to take a few extra minutes to explain to kids the purpose or reason behind what you're asking them to do. Giving reasons works well in any learning setting. When you take time to give reasons, kids appreciate it, learn, and are much more likely to do what you ask of them.

There are times when young people just can't connect what they are asked to do to the reason for doing it, especially when the benefit to them is not immediate or readily apparent. They often fail to realize that good things will happen in the long run if they do what they're asked to do. Giving kids reasons turns on the light bulb that helps them understand the long-term connection. Coaches can use reasons to explain why players do certain drills in practice, why coaches use certain strategies during games, or why youngsters should use character and sportsmanship skills after a defeat. Parents can use reasons to explain why they're asking their child to accept advice or criticism or get along with others.

Whenever you have the opportunity, take time to explain and give reasons. This will help make your life much easier and your teaching and coaching more effective because you've provided kids with immediate "buy-ins." Reasons work, so use them!

Summary

Teaching kids new behaviors and skills so they can learn and change for the better is a very rewarding experience. There are many behaviors and skills you can teach girls and boys in a youth sports setting – physical, social, and character. Situations and youngsters will vary and you'll likely face challenging and difficult times. That's why having the specific behaviors and skills that *Competing with Character* offers, along with proven methods to teach them, are so important to your success with kids. You will have the confidence and knowledge to handle almost anything thrown your way. Teaching new behaviors and skills also gives you the ability to head off problems before they happen and to create an environment where the fun and healthy aspects of youth sports participation are promoted. When this takes place, everyone wins!

CHAPTER

Coaching for Character

Coaches can play a tremendous role in young people's lives. They're important mentors who can influence kids and help them change and grow. Many adults can remember a coach who inspired them and taught valuable lessons that helped them succeed both in and outside of sports, and instilled an appreciation for how athletics enhanced their lives.

Boys and girls stay or leave organized youth sports for different reasons. Coaches and the experiences they provide can often be the factor that determines whether kids continue to play or quit for good. For every person who has positive memories of a coach, there are others who blame a coach for souring their youth sports experience and turning them off from sports and all they offer.

Many coaches involved in youth sports teams, leagues, and clubs are parents who volunteer, and a good number of these parents have little to no coaching experience. For most, the main motivation for getting involved as a coach is to spend time with their child. Most likely, a parent coach played a particular sport in high school and has some knowledge of the game. But having played a sport and knowing how to coach and teach kids how to play it are two different things. This is why it's so important for all youth sports coaches to learn to create and maintain a positive, healthy youth sports setting. And it all starts with priorities – what a coach deems important.

If your main goals as a coach are only about victories, undefeated seasons, championships, and trophies, you're cheating your players and their parents – and yourself – out of a complete sports experience. Only a small number of teams and players are able to win most of their games or a championship trophy. In youth sports, most teams go down in defeat as often as they win. Coaches have to know how to handle winning and losing with class and character, and be able to teach their players (and parents) to do the same.

Emphasizing winning most likely will lead to disappointment for you, your players, and parents. No coach wants to be responsible for turning off a child's interest in athletics. But that's what can happen when it's all about victories and trophies.

Good youth coaches want players and parents to walk away with memories of fun, positive relationships, lasting friendships, and solid lessons learned. They want kids to learn and improve on new skills that can help them in sports and life. They want every player to be excited about playing again the next year. And, you know you've done it right when youngsters and their parents want to play for you again, regardless of your win-loss record or hardware won.

The main goal for any good youth coach is really very simple: to make your kids' athletic experience fun and enjoyable so they want to keep playing and learning. If more coaches had this one simple goal as their top priority, no one would ever lose! And that's where the *Competing with Character* skills and program come in.

Now, we aren't saying winning isn't important. It has its place. But in youth sports, with young girls and boys, it's not at the top of the kids' list, so why should it be at the top of yours? Participating in youth sports is about learning new physical, character, sportsmanship, and life skills, and improving on existing ones. This should be a much higher priority because, as coaches, we only have youngsters for a short time. The worst thing a coach can do is "professionalize" youth sports by making winning and being on top the focus and main goal.

This chapter offers coaches skills – things to do and ways to act – that enable them to set and keep the right priorities. We'll introduce and discuss eight skills coaches can use with players, parents, and fans in their athletic setting. These skills, and their tips for success, will help you create the kind of atmosphere where character and sportsmanship are valued just as much as (and even more than) any victory or trophy.

Do as I Say *and* as I Do

Kids often learn more from your actions than from your words. It's true. Through your actions and reactions, you show kids how to handle positive times with humility, gratitude, and sportsmanship and get through frustrating situations with calmness, good humor, and perseverance.

No one can be a perfect role model all the time. It's natural during the course of a practice or game for your emotions to run high and, at times, get the best of you. After all, you're only human. However, you're more likely to keep your wits about you and your emotions in check when you have a plan and a positive attitude. The *Competing with Character* skills for coaches and tips for success presented in this chapter give you that plan. Using these skills during practices and games and in your interactions with youngsters and parents can help you create a positive, fun environment, successfully deal with difficult situations, and model good character and sportsmanship.

SKILLS FOR COACHES AND TIPS FOR SUCCESS

1. Teach Kids Skills

- Blend the teaching of skills into your practice plan.
- Teach skills before kids face new or difficult situations.
- Look for opportunities to teach, practice, and reinforce skills.

2. Praise and Compliment

- Catch kids being good.
- Praise three times for every correction or criticism (3-to-1 Rule).
- Help kids connect appropriate behavior to desired outcomes.

3. Correct Misbehavior

- Set and stick to your tolerance levels (the line you draw between acceptable and unacceptable behavior).
- Address misbehavior right away; teach to it.
- Give consequences when necessary.

4. Be Organized

- Have a practice plan.
- Keep players busy and reduce idle time.
- Set and work toward goals.

5. Have High Energy

- Motivate yourself.
- Interact with players.
- Be physically active.

6. Model

- Dress like a coach.
- Never use foul language.
- Use proper conduct with players, opponents, and officials.

7. Communicate with Parents

- Let parents know your rules and expectations ahead of time.

- Notify parents of changes or concerns.
- Be empathetic.

8. Understand the Big Picture

- Teach life skills through sports.
- Emphasize competing, not defeating.
- Have fun.

TEACH KIDS SKILLS

A couple of years back, an alumnus who played football for Boys Town decades ago sent me a letter. In it, he told me he had been following my current team and was proud of the success we were having. He also wrote about how the skills and lessons he learned from his former coaches at Boys Town made him the successful businessman and philanthropist he is today. He went on to say these weren't physical skills and lessons he learned from playing football, but instead were the character and life skills he had learned from being part of a team. They included hard work, dedication, perseverance, teamwork, respect for authority, preparation, and others. He took those with him and used them to find success in life.

Learning character and sportsmanship skills from athletics is nothing new. Valuable life lessons have always been part of sports. In youth sports today, however, it seems to have become less and less important to focus on and teach these skills. Character and sportsmanship have been benched in favor of physical performance that can help teams win championships and trophies.

Many youth coaches are good at teaching "playing" skills and helping kids become better athletes. That's a big part of being a successful coach. But it takes a lot more than that to become a *complete* coach. A complete coach teaches the whole package – physical, character, and life skills. This is how young people develop not only as good players but also as well-rounded people who take positive character traits and behaviors to their world outside of sports.

Many coaches in organized youth sports don't grasp the concept of character and life skills teaching. No one has told them the job is more than just helping girls and boys learn how to play a game. For them, it's easier to focus on physical skills because there are so many great resources (mentors, books, clinics, Internet, etc.) available that describe exactly what to teach and what drills to use. It's much more difficult when it comes to teaching character.

We wrote this book to make that part of coaching easier for everyone. The *Competing with Character* skills for players (see page 48) provide exactly what you need to teach in order to promote and develop character and sportsmanship in your players and your sports setting. These skills (which will be discussed in greater detail in Chapter 6, "Playing with Character") form the core of your character development program for youth.

Skills for players range from the basics to those that require young people to work a little harder to learn. Just like with physical skills, it's best to start by teaching the basics like listening, following instructions, accepting feedback, and getting along with others. These allow you to build a foundation where good learning can occur.

Once kids show they can correctly use these basic skills on a regular basis, you can move on to character skills that are more complex – respecting opponents, winning with class and losing with dignity, handling disappointment and adversity, and others.

Skills for Players

1. Listen to Your Coaches
2. Follow Coaches' Instructions
3. Accept Coaching
4. Get Along with Your Teammates
5. Have High Energy
6. Respect Your Opponents
7. Be Prepared for Practices and Games
8. Win with Class and Lose with Dignity
9. Handle Disappointment and Adversity Appropriately
10. Respect Facilities and Equipment

Helping players learn all these skills provides many benefits for you and the kids. Everyone – coaches, players, and parents – knows what is expected, so there are no surprises or confusion about what's acceptable and unacceptable behavior. There's less misbehavior from players and your practices run smoothly. Also, you're more likely to have success in games and see fewer problems and bad behavior from parents. Kids can use these skills to be successful in sports and in other settings like home and school. Finally, others will view you and your team in a positive light because of your commitment to and demonstration of good character and sportsmanship.

Having these skills also takes away any uncertainty about how and what to teach kids regarding character and sportsmanship. When you put the ten skills for players into your coaching toolbox, you can feel confident you're headed in the right direction. There are other behaviors and skills you can teach, and we encourage you to do so. But our main goal is to keep character development as simple, exact, and easy as possible for you, your kids, and their parents. Focus your teaching on these skills for players and you'll soon have an environment where character and sportsmanship are practiced and valued and become second nature.

Blend the Teaching of Skills into Your Practice Plan

Many coaches cringe at the thought of using practice time to do something other than drills and playing skills training. This is understandable because most youth sports coaches have limited practice time. But blending character skills teaching into your practice is easy and takes little time. The first step is making a commitment; then it's all about making it part of your practice plan. This means writing down the skill(s) you plan to review, reinforce, and/or introduce that day, and when and how you'll do the teaching. It's the same planning process you would use for any physical skill or training drill. (We talk about how to develop really effective practice plans later in the chapter.)

In order to run an organized and effective practice, you have to teach youngsters basic skills first. Before you can teach any kind of physical skill or conduct a drill, players need to be able to listen to you, follow your instructions, and accept your feedback and coaching. So, when you first start working with a group of kids, this is where your teaching should begin.

At the first few practices, be prepared to spend a lot of your teaching time reinforcing these basic skills and correcting kids when they don't use them. Also, keep your teaching antenna up. See who listens, follows instructions, and accepts feedback and coaching well and who struggles. Once you've identified the skill level of each youngster, adjust your teaching to meet each child's needs. This means some youngsters will require more time, attention, and teaching from you than other kids. Once your players can correctly use these basic skills on a regular basis, move on to the skills that are a little more advanced.

Teaching character skills to kids usually requires no more than five to ten minutes of your practice time. When you schedule your teaching can vary, depending on your goals. You might put it at the beginning of practice to head off potential problems. Or, you might do it at the end of practice, introducing new skills that players can work on for the next practice or an upcoming game. Let's look at some ways you might blend a few character-building skills for players into your practices.

- At your first practice with a group of young kids who are new to organized sports, you might say something like, *"I'm really excited to be your coach this year and I think we're going to have lots of fun. You're going to learn a lot about soccer. Before we start any of that, though, I want to teach you an important skill called, 'Listen to Your Coaches.' This means that when I'm talking about how to do something or explaining a drill, I expect you to stop what you're doing, look at me, and make an effort to concentrate. When you listen, you'll learn the rules and know how to play the game better, and this will help us be a better team. Any questions?* (Pause. Answer any questions that come up.) *Good. Right now all of you are using this skill really well! Keep it up!"*

- During a previous practice, your players were teasing and arguing with each other. You want to put a stop to further misbehavior. You can talk to the players before practice and say something like, *"Thanks for hustling over. Last practice, there was a lot of teasing and arguing going on and some of you were getting frustrated and upset. We're a team and it's important for all of us to get along and support and encourage one another. So today, let's focus on the skill of getting along with your teammates. You do this by making positive comments and avoiding negative ones, ignoring irritating behaviors, and not making a situation worse by more teasing and arguing. Remember we're all in this together. Do you have any questions?* (Pause for questions.) *Okay. Let's go have a fun practice together!"*

- At the end of practice, you call all the kids together. Once they've gathered around, you might say something like, *"Great practice everyone! You hustled and followed my instructions really well. Keep it up! I want to talk to you about a new skill called 'Respect Facilities and Equipment.' This skill means using the facilities and equipment as they're intended to be used, picking up after yourself and your teammates, and reporting any damage to a coach. This skill can be used at practices and home or away games. It's important to use this skill so other teams and fans see us as positive and respectful, and so we don't have to spend extra money on equipment. Let's start using this*

skill today by picking up the trash in the
dugout and putting away all the equipment.
Any questions? (Pause.) *Great! Let's get started!"*

As you can see, this teaching takes only a little time, but can mean the difference between a successful practice where you accomplish a lot and an unsuccessful one where nothing gets done. Notice also that the coach in these examples gives kids a reason why that particular skill is helpful to them and the team. As always, look for opportunities during practice to reinforce kids when they use skills correctly and to correct misbehavior when it happens. Once you introduce a skill, the best way to help youngsters learn and master it is to capitalize on those spontaneous moments when they try to correctly use the skill and you can praise them or they fall short and need more teaching from you.

When putting together a practice plan, don't limit character teaching to only the start or end of practice. You might decide your teaching will be more effective during a break in the middle of practice. You know your situation and your kids best. Do what works for you, but be sure character teaching is planned and blended into your practices so you won't forget to do it.

Teach Skills Before Kids Face New or Difficult Situations

As mentioned in the previous chapter, Proactive Teaching (or teaching skills before a new or difficult situation arises) is very simple, and it works. In fact, you've probably already had plenty of experience with it. Think about when you've practiced a fire drill, taken driver's education, went through an orientation at work, or took a course like CPR. As a parent, you used it to teach your child how to safely cross the street, dial an emergency phone number, and be careful near a hot stove. In all these situations, the goal is to prepare a person ahead of time for a specific situation so he or she knows what to do when that situation occurs. Knowing what to do helps prevent problems and enables the person to do the right thing.

As a coach, you'll use Proactive Teaching to describe to kids what they should do in a future situation and practice those behaviors in advance. This kind of teaching is most effective when kids are learning something new or when they've had difficulty in past situations. Though it can be used in many areas, it is an especially good tool for helping youngsters learn new, positive ways to respond in situations where they haven't had success in the past.

This teaching approach combines clear messages about what behavior is expected, reasons for using the behavior, and practice (when necessary). Teaching should occur before youngsters face a new situation or a situation where they've had difficulty. It's best to use Proactive Teaching when kids are calm and attentive.

Let's look at an example of how you might use Proactive Teaching in your youth sports setting. Before the first game of the season, you take time at the end of practice to teach a skill to your players: *"Everyone gather around. Great practice! You listened, followed instructions, and hustled really well today. Doing these things in practice will help us in our first game. I want to talk with you about an important skill you'll need to use during games called 'Respect Your Opponents.' This means you don't trash-talk or make rude gestures, you play within the rules, and you ignore any unsportsmanlike behavior from the other team. Using this skill keeps you focused on what you should be doing to help our team. It also helps to make games more fun and not too serious. Let's pretend a player from the other team starts giving you a hard time by saying negative things during the game. What should you do?* (Hands go up, you call on a player, and he answers.) *That's right, Kevin! You ignore it and just keep playing. Most of the time, the person will stop when he sees it's not getting to you. If it really starts bothering you, let me know and I'll talk with the referee. Does anyone have questions? Okay, remember to use this skill and I'll see you at Saturday's game."*

Proactive Teaching works only if you remember to use it. So put it in your practice plan! Don't get discouraged if some kids don't correctly use the skills you teach right away. You might have to practice a skill many times before they understand what you are trying to teach and begin using it consistently. Also, don't expect perfection right away from every kid; some will learn character skills faster than others, just like the physical skills you teach.

When you introduce new skills, you'll do more practice with your kids. Once they're able to correctly and consistently use the skill, you can practice less and just remind kids to use the skill prior to a situation. For example, go back to the previous example where you taught your team to respect their opponents. As your season goes on and your players show they're using the skill correctly, you might say something like this in a pre-game huddle: *"Let's go out and have fun today. Remember to play within the rules, don't trash-talk, and ignore any unsportsmanlike behaviors. Also, let's hustle and encourage one another!"* A quick prompt like this is usually all that's needed to remind kids what you expect of them and help set them up for success.

Look for Opportunities to Teach, Practice, and Reinforce Skills

Every minute you are around your players, there are opportunities to teach and reinforce them for using positive behaviors and skills. It's up to you to pick your teaching moments. Many youth coaches have a hard time with this because they're too focused on playing skills. They miss opportunities to reinforce the really important skills like listening to coaches, accepting coaching, having high energy, and others.

This might seem like one more thing to add to your coaching "to do" list. We know you have many things you want to accomplish during practices that can sometimes bump teaching and reinforcing positive character behaviors and skills down the priority list. Some coaches even think this is outside their coaching duties. Actually, this teaching is probably a coach's most important responsibility. Teaching players what you expect from them reduces misbehavior during practices so they run smoother and actually lets you get more done.

A common mistake youth coaches make is to confuse "preaching" with teaching. Preaching involves lecturing youngsters, pounding them with the same thing over and over in the hope that they learn and change. If you've done this, you probably know it's not an effective way to work with kids and get things accomplished. Teaching involves describing specific behavior so kids understand what you're talking about and what you expect from them. When youngsters do something right or use a skill correctly, tell them exactly what they did and praise them for it so they keep doing it. For example, if you see your players ignoring unsportsmanlike behaviors from their opponents during a game, you might say something like, *"Guys, I like the way you're not getting involved in the trash talking going on out there. Just keep ignoring it and continue to play hard. Good job!"* Or, if you observe a player showing high energy during practice, you might say something like, *"Great hustle out there! You're running from drill to drill and giving maximum effort. That's how you get better and help the team. Keep up the good work!"*

Teaching also can involve consequences that help motivate kids to learn and change. When kids display positive behaviors and skills, you can reinforce and strengthen them even more by giving positive consequences. These can range from verbal praise to more concrete rewards like treats or helmet stickers. Just remember that youngsters will respond differently to certain rewards; what works with one kid might not work with another. For example, some kids love to be praised in front of their teammates, while others get embarrassed and respond better to a private pat on the back from you. Know what positive consequences work with each one of your kids and tailor your teaching and rewards to match his or her needs.

Kids and adults want to be part of a positive and upbeat environment, whether it's youth sports, school, home, work, or some other setting. Looking for opportunities to teach and reinforce appropriate behaviors and skills is your tool for creating this kind of atmosphere. Young people are more likely to choose and use positive behaviors and skills when they know you value them. Always be on the lookout for the appropriate use of any positive behavior or skill – character, social, or physical. If you've done your job well, you'll see kids using them all the time. Then, be ready to praise their efforts! This might seem strange at first but when you see the positive reactions of your young people and the positive results, you'll wonder how you ever got along without it!

PRAISE AND COMPLIMENT

Many activities compete for kids' attention today. Youngsters have lots of options for how to spend their free time – the Internet, video and computer games, TV, movies, and others. These activities have value and can be good for kids. But youth sports are unique; the opportunity to be physically fit and to learn and play a game offers them extremely meaningful and enriching experiences that last a lifetime. In a real way, sports are competing for kids' time and attention. So if we want girls and boys to benefit from all youth sports have to offer, we have to make it appealing.

Youngsters choose to be involved in an activity because it's fun. Nobody wants to participate in something that's not enjoyable. When coaches focus on the positives and spend a majority of their time praising, complimenting, and encouraging young people, practices and games are much more pleasant for kids and adults.

I learned this the hard way with one of my Boys Town football teams. One year, we had more than our share of negative incidents with some players, both on and off the field. It was disappointing, frustrating, and distracting. I reacted by falling back into a "critique-and-criticize" coaching mode. In other words, I focused more on what the players did wrong than what they did right, which is not how I normally coach. As a result, the players and coaches weren't as upbeat as usual and they gradually lost enthusiasm and energy as the season progressed. We had a successful win-loss season, but it wasn't much fun. Players and coaches became frustrated and the team never gelled or reached its potential. At the end of the season, players and coaches were worn out and just ready for the year to be done.

That year, I failed to make the game of football enjoyable for our kids. When that happened, many players were not willing to invest themselves in the hard work it takes to build a great team. After a while, they began tuning out the coaches and just coasted to the season's end. The valuable lesson I learned is that coaches at any level must always strive to keep the game fun and enjoyable for kids. When we don't, everybody loses.

Praising and complimenting youngsters is another one of those skills youth coaches should learn and put in their coaching toolbox. Before coming to Boys Town, I expected kids to do things the right way, and I spent most of my time telling players and students what they were doing wrong. Today, thanks to what I've learned and experienced at Boys Town, I've switched gears; now I focus on praising, complimenting, and encouraging young people. They respond much better to a positive approach, and everything about playing the game is just more enjoyable for everyone.

Many youth sports coaches would be surprised if they could see a videotape of how they interact with their players. Coaches would likely see many more negative interactions than positive ones. This isn't because they consciously choose to be negative. It's usually because they don't recognize just how powerful praise and reinforcement can be with youngsters. Once coaches understand this, put it into action, and see the results, they're sold on the power of praise.

The reality is that all girls and boys who play youth sports will make lots of mistakes, so there will always be lots to correct. That's okay – it's all part of the learning process. But to make your coaching truly effective, so young people learn *and have fun,* you have to praise, compliment, and encourage.

Now that you know the value of praise and compliments, here's one more important point: You must be genuine and sincere when praising young people. If you just go through the motions by randomly telling your players *"Good job"* or *"Way to go"* with little enthusiasm, they'll come to see you and your praise as phony and insincere. This can harm relationships and erode the trust your kids have in you. So, when using praise, be specific about what children did to earn it and tell them in a way that shows you mean it. Look them in the eye, smile, use an upbeat and positive voice tone, and choose words that tell kids you're proud of them.

Catch Kids Being Good

Our motto, "Catch 'em being good!", means going out of your way to look for and praise positive behaviors. It doesn't mean ignoring negative behavior, but instead finding a balance where you praise more than you correct kids.

Pay attention to the positive things young people do, no matter how small or insignificant they might seem. A lot of coaches praise only the major accomplishments like scoring a touchdown, hitting a home run, or winning a race. But positive little things are going to occur much more often, and they deserve your praise as well. When kids behave properly, use skills correctly, take the right action, or make good decisions, notice and reward them for it! This will motivate them to keep up their good work. Praise, reinforcement, and positive consequences help kids choose the best course of action.

Being on the lookout opens up lots of opportunities to praise, compliment, and encourage players during practices and games. When a youngster follows your instruction to pick up the volleyballs, you can say something like, *"Nice job! Thanks for picking up the volleyballs right when I asked you."* Or, when players arrive on time to a baseball game with all their equipment, you could say, *"Way to go guys! You all have your gloves and bats and you're here in plenty of time to warm up. Let's go have some fun!"* When your focus is on praising kids, there are unlimited opportunities to be positive by pointing out what they are doing right.

Praise Three Times for Every Correction or Criticism (3-to-1 Rule)

With some kids and in certain situations, it can be difficult to find things to praise. You might have a player or two who rubs you the wrong way because he or she misbehaves or consistently struggles with the most basic drills and skills. This can be frustrating for you and the kids. However, it's still your responsibility to catch them being good at something. You might have to work a bit harder to find things to praise but it will be worth it. Even the smallest amount of praise and encouragement can make all the difference in a youngster's sports experience.

At Boys Town, we follow the "3-to-1 Rule" with our players. This means that for every negative consequence or correction a player earns for inappropriate behavior, we look for at least three opportunities to praise and reinforce the youth for a positive behavior. (With some players, the ratio can be even higher if the individual needs lots of encouragement to keep trying to improve.) For example, a youth baseball coach might tell a player who strikes out most of the time: *"Great job of swinging only at strikes* (praise)*! You fouled off a couple of good pitches and got it to a full count* (praise)*. I liked the way you remembered to use the stance we've been working on* (praise)*, and you swung on time* (praise)*. Next time, be sure to watch the ball as it comes across the plate* (correction)*. You'll get 'em next time* (encouragement)*!"*

The biggest advantage of using the 3-to-1 Rule in a youth sports setting is that it forces you to focus on the positive and remain encouraging. This helps create an upbeat atmosphere for you and the players. Also, players and parents tend to catch on and become more supportive and encouraging toward you and each other.

Help Kids Connect Appropriate Behavior to Desired Outcomes

Boys and girls don't always understand that what they are doing today can affect what happens to them in the immediate or distant future. Most of the time, their focus is on the here and now. It's difficult for many kids, especially younger ones, to see how certain behaviors and skills can help them reach goals and succeed. So it's important for you to take time to explain to young people why you're asking them to do certain things in specific ways. When you give youngsters compelling reasons, they're more likely to buy into what you want them to do and do it without complaining.

As we said, the best way to teach appropriate skills and behaviors is to keep the spotlight on the positive! Teach youngsters what they should do or continue doing and not what they shouldn't do. Then, tie it all together by connecting positive behaviors and skills to future success.

Every year, I share with my players what successful players and teams did correctly in the past. I explain exactly what actions they took and how their positive behaviors and skills resulted in desired outcomes. This helps my current players understand what it takes and what they need to do to create a successful team and season for themselves.

While I do mention the physical skills related to sports, I spend most of my time talking about character, sportsmanship, and social skills. For example, explaining to players how a character skill like getting along with teammates can help them and the team succeed is every bit as important (and probably more!) as diagramming and working on a drill for practice or a play for a game.

It's important for kids to be able to connect all the skills you teach to desired outcomes and goals, on the field and off. We want youngsters to walk away from the time they spend with us feeling good about themselves and what they've accomplished. This helps them connect and apply what they learn in sports to other areas of their lives and understand how these skills can be of value at school, at home, and in their relationships with others.

As we know, when sports stop being enjoyable, kids stop participating. The good news is you have a lot of control over creating a positive and pleasant atmosphere where young people can learn, grow, and change. When you focus on catching kids being good, use lots of praise when they do things right, and stress the positive over the negative, you can make your sports setting one that you and your youngsters want to come back to.

Praise and compliments lift kids up, make them want to try harder, and get them excited and eager to play at practices and games. Enjoyment comes from knowing that someone notices their efforts to try hard and get better. It's a great feeling when you see kids smile because you told them they did something well.

CORRECT MISBEHAVIOR

Working with young people isn't for the faint of heart. Even if sports are fun for kids and something they enjoy doing, it doesn't mean they won't misbehave. At practices and games, there will be problems, negative behaviors, and mistakes you'll have to deal with. Part of being a successful coach is being able to address and correct youth misbehavior in a positive and constructive way.

Coaches must be willing and know how to handle youngsters when they become frustrated, disappointed, angry, and sad. This isn't always an easy or pleasant thing to do. Many times, these strong emotions can lead kids to react with nasty and inappropriate words and actions toward you and others. So it's important for you to have teaching tools that can help you coach kids to learn better, more appropriate ways to act and react in emotionally charged situations.

Turning a blind eye to misbehavior isn't a good option. Ignoring negative behaviors leads to bigger problems or, at least, more of the same kind of problems. For example, if you allow players to talk when you're talking, you'll have a group of poor listeners who interfere with your teaching. If you allow it to continue, you'll grow more and more frustrated, and gradually start to treat and interact with your players in a negative way.

The best way to handle misbehaviors is to see them as learning opportunities for kids. We usually learn more from our mistakes and failures than we do from our successes. Problem behaviors are fertile teaching opportunities for youngsters to learn valuable lessons. When you adopt this kind of outlook and approach, you turn a bad situation into something positive. When you view misbehavior as a hassle and an irritating distraction, you're likely to treat young people like that too – and nothing good comes from it.

Never assume that kids know a skill and how to use it properly – even the most basic ones. Children don't come into the world knowing how to follow instructions, listen, and accept feedback. They learn these skills from adults who take the time to teach them. And youngsters need to learn how to correctly use skills in different settings like school and athletics.

It's also important not to take misbehavior and mistakes personally. Sometimes, this is hard to do because kids will say things in the heat of the moment that can anger or frustrate you. You might hear statements like *"You're not fair!"* or *"You don't like me!"* When young people do this, they're trying to take the focus off their negative behavior and get you sidetracked to issues that are irrelevant. Don't take the bait! Instead, continue with your teaching and keep your focus on correcting their specific misbehavior.

Part of a kid's job is to test your limits. They'll poke and prod to see if you'll really do something about unacceptable behaviors. When limits are tested and misbehavior happens, your job is to calmly and consistently address the misbehavior and teach kids what to do instead. Not taking misbehavior personally goes a long way toward helping you do this. The last thing you want to do is lose your cool, get upset, and make the situation worse.

Correcting misbehavior involves telling youngsters what they did wrong and what to do right the next time, and giving a consequence. Following this winning formula helps kids learn from their mistakes and succeed in future situations.

When you calmly and appropriately address and correct misbehavior, everyone wins. You get a smooth-running and productive setting because kids know what you expect from them and what behaviors are acceptable and unacceptable. And when youngsters understand you mean business, they're more likely to settle down, have fun, and follow the rules.

Set and Stick to Your Tolerance Levels

A big part of successfully dealing with misbehavior is establishing low tolerance levels with your players from the beginning and consistently keeping them in place with teaching. Tolerance levels define the behaviors you deem to be acceptable or unacceptable. Setting a low tolerance means you do not allow much negative behavior to go by without teaching and correcting it. Keeping your tolerances low is the best way to work with young people in any setting.

Low tolerances help you create an environment where players are more likely to listen, follow instructions, and accept feedback. Misbehavior decreases as youth come to learn that positive behaviors are valued and reinforced. This allows you to get more done during practices and keeps the focus on teaching skills.

It doesn't take long for kids to figure out what they can and can't get away with. That's why it's so important for you to set the tone right away. This means taking time before you begin working with youngsters to develop and establish your expectations for them. Write these down and review them with your players at the first practice. Clearly spell out what's acceptable during practices and games and what isn't, along with possible consequences. Once you've laid this foundation, it's up to you to stick to these expectations and follow through with teaching when they aren't met.

Let's look at an example of how this works with our football players at Boys Town. The very first day of practice, we stress the importance of being on time. We explain to players our expectations, why it's important, and the negative consequences for being late. This is all taught beforehand, so it's up to the players to follow through. If they aren't on time (and I mean to the minute!), they earn a negative consequence – flipping a tractor tire one hundred yards in a certain amount of time – before they can enter practice. At the start of the season, some players usually test the limits by arriving a few seconds or minutes late. But once they see we mean business, they're rarely late again.

Address Misbehavior Right Away; Teach to It

When problem behaviors happen, the sooner you address and correct them the better. This helps kids make the connection between their negative behavior and what happens as a result. If you wait too long to address misbehavior, letting it go on before you act, kids will wonder why it "suddenly" became wrong. Acting right away shows other youngsters that you're serious about not allowing certain behaviors and that you're sticking to the tolerances you set. When you ignore misbehavior or let kids off the hook, you end up with a group of players who will regularly test the limits to see if this is the time they can get away with something.

The way to teach to misbehavior is to tell kids what they did wrong, tell them exactly what to do differently next time, and use a consequence (if necessary). This teaching doesn't take much time and is crucial to building a sports setting that's successful, positive, and fun for you and the players. Let's look at some examples of how you can address and correct misbehavior when it happens:

- You instruct a group of girls at a basketball practice to do a dribbling drill they've been taught and know how to do. One girl starts shooting at a basket. You might say something like, *"Jackie, I understand you're excited about shooting the basketball, but right now we're working on dribbling. You're not following instructions. When you follow instructions, we get more done and can get to things you want to do, like shooting. When I give you an instruction, you need to listen closely, do what I say right away and with energy, and raise your hand and ask questions if you don't understand. Does that make sense?* (Jackie says, "Yes.") *Good. Remember to do that for the rest of practice."*

- A player has struggled in soccer practice to "head" a ball. You pull the player aside to teach him how to do it correctly. When you do, he snaps, *"I know how to do this! Let me do it again."* You might say something like, *"It's great that you want to try again. But right now, you're not accepting my coaching. When I give you suggestions, I expect you to follow them right away without talking back. If you're frustrated, let me know and we can work things out. Remember that coaches are just trying to help you get better. Do you have any questions? Okay, great. Now, let's go over how to safely head the ball again, and I want you to remember what we just talked about."*

- After a loss, one of your players slams his hockey stick on the bench. You might say something like, *"Bobby, I know losing can be difficult, but slamming your stick against the bench isn't an acceptable way to handle disappointment and adversity. When tough things happen in games and practice, you're expected not to use negative physical or verbal behaviors, learn from the situation, and work harder. Doing this helps you and your teammates get better. Do you understand?* (Bobby nods his head and apologizes.) *Thanks for saying you're sorry. Now, your consequence for slamming your stick is to pick up all the equipment on the bench and put it away before you leave."*

Give Consequences When Necessary

When kids misbehave, you can motivate them to use positive behavior in the future by giving negative consequences. Usually, the best negative consequence for youngsters in youth sports is to have them sit out a certain amount of time in practice or a game. They want to play, and taking playing time away usually is enough to get their attention. For some kids, you might have them do something they don't enjoy, like jogging a lap or two. If you do use a physical consequence, make sure it's not too harsh or overly demanding, like having a youth run the entire practice or do a hundred pushups.

Always use the smallest negative consequence that will result in a behavior change. In other words, don't use a big consequence when a smaller one will do the job. For example, if correcting a child in front of his or her peers is enough to change that child's behavior, don't add on laps or sitting out. In this situation, being corrected in front of the team is just enough to get the job done.

Consequences work as long as they are individualized. This means you have to know what works with each player. Kids are different and unique, and some respond differently to the same consequence. Some kids might not think jogging around the field is a big deal but dread having to sit out during practice or a game. So get to know your kids and use the consequences that work for each one.

Never humiliate a player in the name of giving a consequence. It's natural to become frustrated and even angry with some youngsters, especially when they continually misbehave. But it's your job to stay calm and use teaching along with fair and humane negative consequences to correct problem behaviors.

As a youth sports coach, you'll see your share of misbehavior and mistakes when kids try to use various skills. This comes with the territory and is part of the learning process for kids. Good coaching involves helping young people learn from their mistakes and learn new ways to behave and grow as athletes and people. To do this, establish your tolerances early and stick to them. When you see misbehavior, address and teach to it right away. Give negative consequences if the situation warrants, but be careful not to go overboard. Correcting misbehavior in these ways allows you to develop and maintain an environment where kids aren't afraid to make mistakes because they trust you and know you will respond firmly but fairly.

BE ORGANIZED

Athletics demand physical effort as well as focus and attention from participants. Expending physical and mental energy wears athletes down. With boys and girls in youth sports, this can happen quickly; kids can lose interest and their attention can start to drift, especially during practices. This is why being able to organize practices is such an important skill for coaches. You want to put together a plan of attack that holds kids' attention, keeps them moving, and motivates them.

Have a Practice Plan

Many youth sports practices are not as well organized as they could be. It's usually not because coaches lack commitment or motivation, but because they don't know how to set up a practice that keeps kids engaged and learning. Don't expect a positive outcome with your players if you just go out and "wing it" in practice. The best way to enhance your teaching and youth learning is to develop good practice plans.

Kids know organization when they see it. When someone is in charge, teaching and directing players from one drill or activity to the next, they respond positively. Well-run practices play a big role in skill mastery and improved performance. A well-prepared practice plan also reduces the opportunity kids have to misbehave or goof around.

A practice plan is simply an outline written by the coach that lists everything that will happen during practice (see the example practice plan on page 72). It includes the drills and activities you'll use, how long you'll spend on them, how you're going to teach them, and the equipment you'll need. A good practice plan reduces idle time, youth misbehavior, and frustration by coaches and participants, distractions that can take away from teaching and learning.

When developing a practice plan, be as detailed as possible. Describe the exact drills, tasks, and activities you'll use and how you'll teach them. It's also important to determine the specific amount of time you'll need for each drill or practice segment. For example, you might spend five minutes warming up, six minutes stretching, ten minutes on your first drill, eight minutes on your second drill, and so on. Stick to those times and you'll get a lot accomplished in the time you have (usually an hour for young athletes).

Drills and activities should be specific to one physical skill at a time (for example, the toss for an overhand volleyball serve or the correct footwork for a basketball layup). Don't teach everything at once. Overloading kids with too much information and too many instructions is a sure-fire recipe for failure. Instead, break each physical skill down into its most basic components and teach these individually. Then, step by step, build from there until youngsters can work on the entire physical skill.

Sample Practice Plan

Flag Football Practice

Time & Drill Session	Coach Jones	Coach Smith	Parent Volunteer	Parent Volunteer

5:00 – 5:10 pm Introductions	• Coach and player introductions
	• Behavior expectations
	• Preteach these two skills:
	   "Listen to Your Coaches"
	   "Follow Coaches' Instructions"
	
	Goals for practice: Fun & Respect			

5:10 – 5:22 pm Skill Stations Three minutes per station	**Giving & Receiving a Handoff**	**Passing** • Two hands on ball • Take ball to launch point • Belly button at target	**Catching** • Thumbs together above waist; pinkies together below waist • LOOK, REACH, CATCH, LOCK	**Receiver Stance** and get-off
5:22 – 5:25 pm Break and Drink				
5:25 – 5:35 pm Angle Tackle	**Coaching Points** • Aim for the hip • Keep wide base • Eyes on flag	• Start drill on "hut" • End drill on whistle		
5:35 – 6:00 pm	• Explain alignment • Walk though base play	• Watch center position		

Announcements	• Next practice Sunday at 5 pm
	• Get mouth guard and football shoes
	• Review these two skills:
	   "Listen to Your Coaches"
	   "Follow Coaches' Instructions"			

Keep drills short. Young people lose interest in drill periods that last longer than ten or fifteen minutes. When youngsters get bored, misbehavior starts; keep them moving from one drill to the next. That way, kids only have to keep their focus for short periods of time and they get the repetitions they need to improve the physical skill you're teaching.

A great way to learn how to develop a successful practice plan is to visit with a high school coach. You'll find that a lot of upper level coaches are extremely accommodating to young or inexperienced coaches seeking advice and help. They remember being in your position and having a coaching mentor who assisted them. Ask the coach for help in drawing up a practice plan that will work well for you and your youngsters. Most coaches will suggest simple and easy-to-instruct drills and activities that focus on the fundamentals. They'll also encourage you to stay away from anything too complicated.

When visiting with the coach, ask if you can watch one of his or her practices. To the untrained eye, it might look jumbled but it's really choreographed very carefully. While there, you can get lots of great ideas on drills and how to organize, develop, and use your practice plan. Model your practices after what works at these practices.

Finally, allow yourself plenty of time to put a practice plan together. Avoid making it up on the run or scribbling it down five minutes before practice starts. For my high school football team, I usually spend two hours every day developing a practice plan. For youth sports, allow yourself thirty to sixty minutes to prepare.

Organization helps kids build trust and confidence in you and your ability to get the job done. Leave no stone unturned in your preparation. You'll be amazed at how much you accomplish when you prepare and plan your practices. They will run smoother, kids will learn better, and all of you will have much more fun!

Keep Players Busy and Reduce Idle Time

Idle time during practice is one of the top problems for many youth sports coaches, especially inexperienced coaches. Most times, it involves players standing around in lines waiting their turn during drills. At some practices, kids spend more time watching and waiting than actually moving and doing something physical. This is a recipe for disaster. It leads to inattention and boredom, which can result in player misbehavior and poor learning.

The best way to easily fix this problem is to have an assistant coach help you at practice. Lots of youth coaches try to teach and run practices by themselves with ten, fifteen, or more players. This is too many kids for one person. Using an assistant coach lets you split up the youngsters into manageable numbers and run several drills at once. This keeps activity flowing and players moving from one drill to the next. More repetitions lead to more effective and successful teaching and learning.

Don't be afraid to ask parents for help. Many are willing to get involved, and it doesn't take long to show a volunteer parent exactly what he or she needs to do to lead kids in a drill. Remember to keep the drill and teaching simple so parents don't get confused.

Make sure parents understand their role. Remind them they are there to help you run an up-tempo practice with lots of movement from drill to drill. Ask them to work within the boundaries you give them. If they need help with a drill or if players are misbehaving, ask them to come to you. Remember, you're in charge; never put a volunteer parent in a difficult or compromising situation.

Get commitments from parents ahead of time and outline their roles and responsibilities. That way, you can list who is teaching what drill or activity in your practice plan. Avoid looking for parents to help minutes before practice starts.

Set and Work Toward Goals

Practices and practice plans should be driven by your goals. These goals should include teaching the skills and lessons you want your players to learn and match your team's or organization's philosophies and goals. Some youth sports teams and organizations claim they focus on teaching the fundamentals of a sport. But when you observe their practices, they actually spend more time on team drills like running plays or scrimmaging. Team drills have their place, but they should take a back seat to having players become proficient in the fundamentals.

It takes a strong commitment to stay focused on your goals. Sometimes, coaches get bored teaching fundamentals. They want to move on too quickly to activities that are more exciting and challenging, like team drills, scrimmages, and strategy. Some new coaches might even think that teaching fundamentals isn't really helping the players at all. That's why some creativity might go a long way toward keeping practices fun and interesting for the kids.

When setting goals for practice, never assume players know how to do something. It's better to assume they don't know how to do certain skills, even the most basic ones. You will rarely go wrong by starting with or at least reviewing the basics.

In youth sports, you'll coach kids with varying athletic, physical, and learning skills. Some youngsters will be miles ahead, while others will just be getting started. Starting with the fundamentals puts all players on an equal footing and gives them the opportunity to learn from the ground up. Once your players can perform the basic skills pretty well, you can move onto more advanced skills.

Besides reducing the frustration level of coaches and helping practices run smoother, being organized teaches and models the importance of preparation and time management. When players see that their coaches are in control and have practices planned out, they will have more confidence in their coaches and what they're teaching. This means better learning and more fun for everyone!

HAVE HIGH ENERGY

As a coach, the energy and enthusiasm you bring to your youth sports setting sets the tone for your team and your individual players. If you want them to hustle and be positive, upbeat, and motivated, then do all those things yourself. When you model high energy for youngsters, you're more likely to get it back from them.

Many youth coaches don't understand what high energy means. It's not about being loud or yelling. It's not about sideline dramatics that coaches think will fire up their players. People get this misconception from watching professional and college coaches on TV who complain and scream at officials and players, or throw tantrums after the game while being interviewed by the media. This kind of behavior isn't acceptable at any level, especially youth sports. It creates a negative atmosphere where kids are uncomfortable, tentative, and afraid to make mistakes.

Coaches with high energy are upbeat, positive, and motivating. They are teachers and cheerleaders for young players, encouraging them to keep improving and striving to reach their goals. They're excited and happy to be at practice and ooze a love for the sport. And they work diligently to help pass their high energy on to players.

Every day at practice, my coaches and I demonstrate high energy; some days, it's needed more than others. This is especially true after the fourth or fifth day of two-a-day football practices. This is a rough part of the pre-season training schedule when many players need a pick-me-up. They are tired and sore, and their enthusiasm and energy is fading. So, I do things to help keep practices loose, upbeat, and fun. For example, I'll put a rubber snake on the practice field before an early morning practice. During practice, my assistant coaches and I pretend to stumble over it. The players get a kick out of the joke, almost instantly perk up, and work with more energy and enthusiasm. You can do similar things to help keep kids alert and excited.

Motivate Yourself

High energy is something all coaches can control. It has nothing to do with coaching experience or a team's talent level. The energy and enthusiasm you bring to practices and games is something you can turn on whenever you choose to.

Having a high energy level helps kids build trust in you. When they see you are working hard to help them, they're more likely to work hard for you because they know it's something you value. When you demonstrate enthusiasm, energy, and hustle, you set an example youngsters are more likely to follow.

I put this to the test a few years ago with my football team. The team was dragging, practicing with very low energy and enthusiasm. They were almost apathetic toward drills and other activities. After a couple of practices, I decided to mirror their low energy level in my coaching. I acted disinterested, wasn't upbeat or vocal, and didn't pass on much encouragement. Basically, I stayed pretty quiet. It didn't take long for players to notice something was different and ask what was wrong. I took this opportunity to talk with them about how important it is for everyone on the team to display high energy. The players understood and agreed to start working harder during practices.

It's impossible for people to remain upbeat and enthusiastic all the time. There are times when we just don't feel like showing high energy; it's part of being human. I tell my players it happens to me and it will happen to them. When it does, I tell them how many people deal with it: They "fake it."

Every day, there are people who go to work with low energy. They might feel a bit ill, have a problem at home, or tossed and turned through a sleepless night. These are reasons – not excuses – for why people might not have much get-up-and-go that day. Under most circumstances in the workplace, people are still expected to come in, do their jobs the best they can, and be pleasant and positive toward others. Even on the bad days, I expect these same things from my players and coaches – and myself. So should you!

So, when your energy level is low, fake it. Do your best to be reinforcing and enthusiastic for the hour or so you're with kids in practices or at games. Don't bring your troubles to the fields and courts. That's not fair to the kids and it just creates confusion and tension.

As a youth sports coach, it's important for you to come to practices and games motivated and ready to go. The good news is that most youth sports coaches have little problem doing this. Even after a difficult day at work or home, coaching and teaching a sport they are passionate about is a great way to relax and have fun.

Interact with Players

When I first started coaching, I would stand in front of my players as they stretched at the beginning of practice. I soon realized I was interacting – making eye contact, shouting encouragement, and just talking – with only a handful of players in the first couple of rows. So my assistant coaches and I made it a point to move around and visit with every player – front, middle, and back lines. This helped build higher energy in players and the team and improved relationships.

It's important for all young people to know you care about them, regardless of their talent level. Often, players who lack natural talent or struggle don't get as much of a coach's time and attention. When that happens, these kids can feel isolated and lonely and practices or games aren't much fun for them.

This is why coaches should spend some time with each of their players. It doesn't have to be anything elaborate or involve deep conversations about life. You can do simple things like ask about their day, school activities, and other extracurricular activities (music, movies, etc.); crack a joke and laugh with them; or give them words of praise and encouragement. These little interactions help youngsters feel good and know you care.

During practice, avoid standing around barking out orders. Instead, move around, converse with players, and work at improving your relationships with them. This is the area where coaches have their greatest impact on kids. Most players won't become great at the sport you're coaching, but all can benefit from the time, attention, praise, and encouragement you give them. You'll be remembered more for doing these things than for the physical skills you taught.

Remember, make it a priority to spend time getting to know every youngster on your team. Kids come to youth sports from varied backgrounds and with unique experiences. You might provide the only positive adult interaction a child has that day. When you take the time to talk and connect with kids, it means a lot to them. For many kids in youth sports, this might be the best part of their youth sports experience.

Be Physically Active

Coaching is a job that requires action. Most of the time, you're doing things like hustling around with players from drill to drill or demonstrating how to do a physical skill. So be prepared to be physically active, especially during practices.

Remember that kids pick up on what you model for them. When you demonstrate high energy and hustle, they're more likely to do these things in practice and games. Also, when you have fun while being active, youngsters are more likely to be upbeat and positive about it too. This can lead to less complaining and more effort during drills in practice.

Being energetic and active in your youth sports setting is great for your mind and body. It helps you keep your energy level high and relieves the stress that can come from coaching and working with young people. It's also a great way to blow off steam so you can be patient, calm, and positive when you work with youngsters.

Having high energy teaches kids how to work hard, be enthusiastic, build relationships, keep fit, and have fun. Young people can put these skills to good use in many other parts of their lives. One of the best ways for them to learn these things is through your example and actions. Your behavior and actions set the tone for practices and games. When you're upbeat, positive, and enthusiastic, you'll find the kids are too!

MODEL

During one of my son's youth sports practices, I saw the head coach take out a can of chewing tobacco and put a wad in his mouth – right in front of the kids! This might not seem like a big deal to many coaches, but it is. Today, too many adults think it's okay to use unhealthy, inappropriate, or bad behavior around kids. The problem is that coaches and parents tend to downplay these incidents, or simply don't understand the significance and influence their behavior has on young people.

One of the important things you must do as a coach is be aware of what you say and do around your players. You set the tone for how youngsters and parents behave and respond during practices and games. Most of them will follow your lead, adopting and copying what you do. When you display good character and sportsmanship behaviors and skills, players, parents, and fans are likely to do the same.

Since youngsters watch and learn from you, it's important to carefully and wisely choose your words and actions. When you sign up to be a youth coach, you also sign on to be a role model. Being aware of and accepting this is the first step toward becoming the best model you can be for your players and their parents. A role model is a person who shows kids, through what he or she says and does, how to do the right thing in various situations. In youth sports, coaches and parents are the important role models kids look to for direction. It goes with the territory and is something you can't minimize or escape.

Unfortunately, today's media highlights and often sensationalizes bad behavior by coaches and athletes in college and professional sports. These coaches and athletes – whether they believe it or not – are role models for kids. Kids see these adults trash talking, arguing with officials, fighting, and showboating on television and think it's perfectly okay for them to do the same. This is why it's so important for youth coaches at the grassroots level to emphasize, teach, and show kids the importance of and how to use good character and sportsmanship skills. Young people already see plenty of what not to do; they need to learn what **to do**. And you're in the unique position to help them do that.

It's a difficult task to gain kids' trust, earn their respect, and get positive results when you take a "do as I say, not as I do" approach to coaching. Kids won't buy into your messages or accept your coaching when you say one thing and do another. You have to live what you preach and teach. When you have to cover your tracks because you've behaved inappropriately, youngsters will lose their respect for and trust in you. So strive to be a coach who not only teaches and talks about good character but also lives it.

Modeling is an "all-the-time" thing. It's not something you turn on and off or do every now and then. If it's not a natural part of you and your coaching, kids will eventually see through the facade. It's only human for people to slip up and display poor behavior. When it happens to you, use it as a great opportunity to demonstrate for kids what they should do when they make a mistake: Admit and own your behavior, make amends, and correct any wrongs. Not only is this great modeling, but it's also the right thing to do. How you respond to your mistakes will have a powerful effect on how your kids respond to theirs.

Dress Like a Coach

At any youth sports practice, it should be clear who the coach is simply by how he or she is dressed. You should look the part, and this means dressing in a way that shows you are in charge and take the job of coaching kids seriously. What you choose to wear also is a big part of being a good role model. When you look like a coach, players and parents take you more seriously and buy into you and what you're teaching more quickly.

Always remember that you're representing not only yourself but also your players, parents, fans, and, in many cases, an entire organization. So, during practices and games, you should be neatly groomed and appropriately dressed. Wear a shirt or hat that displays the team or organization name. This helps promote and build a sense of pride and togetherness that's part of every good team. Also, since coaches are active, wear pants (or shorts) and shoes that are neat and comfortable and allow you to easily interact and get physically involved with the players, especially during practices.

Avoid clothing that advertises or is connected to alcohol, drugs, or sex. It's not uncommon to see a youth coach wearing a hat or shirt with a beer or tobacco logo or advertisement on it. This kind of dress reflects poorly on you and sends the wrong message to young people. It also allows these companies to use you to promote their products to kids.

It's easy to spot coaches who take their job seriously; they dress the part. Parents and kids have much more trust and confidence in a person who dresses in a professional manner. And this starts the first time they meet you. First impressions carry a lot of weight, and just like in a job interview, people will make up their minds about you and your abilities based on that first meeting. How you look and what you wear plays a huge role in making a good first impression with players and parents. So dress appropriately from the get-go! It helps get everything off to a good start.

At Boys Town, we have a dress code for all our football coaches. On Monday, Wednesday, and Friday, we wear blue (school color) shirts that are plain or have a Boys Town logo or design on them, along with light pants.

On Tuesday and Thursday, we do the opposite: light tops and dark pants. All coaches are held accountable to this dress code. The players notice what we wear and comment that the coaches all dress alike. We tell them we're a team and proud to be Cowboy football coaches. This attitude trickles down to our players, who also take great satisfaction in wearing Cowboy football gear that lets people know they're members of the football team.

If your team or organization doesn't pay for coaches' gear, go out and buy it yourself. You don't have to spend a lot of money; just get a T-shirt or two (and possibly a hat) made with your team name on it. Wear this clothing at all practices and games. The little money you spend on these items will go a long way toward promoting and developing unity and pride in your team.

Never Use Foul Language

Some coaches equate the use of foul language with intensity. They think cursing or using inappropriate language is a way to emphasize a point, get kids' attention, fire up the team, or get players to give more effort. This couldn't be further from the truth. Yes, intensity is a big part of being successful in competition, but you don't need to use inappropriate words or phrases to create it. Foul language simply has no place in youth sports.

Remember that parents are entrusting you with their most sacred gift – their children. They're expecting you to build an environment that's constructive, positive, and appropriate. When you use foul language, kids are likely to use it too, whether it's at practice, a game, home, or school. The last thing you want is for parents to tell you that their child said he or she learned negative language from you.

A good rule of thumb is to talk to your players as you would want an adult to talk to your own kids. Before you say something to a child, especially when you're frustrated or upset, ask yourself if the words you're about to use are suitable for your own kids. You wouldn't want someone cursing at or using other inappropriate language with your child, and neither do your players' parents. So keep your language clean and constructive.

There might be a time when you slip up and use foul language. It happens to the best of us. And it's more likely to happen during difficult or emotional times at practices and games. This is when it's most important for you to keep your words positive and appropriate. This models for kids how to respond and behave during difficult situations. Look at a slip as a teachable moment when you can admit your mistake, apologize, and learn. This shows kids what they should do when they make mistakes.

When parents or fans use improper language in the stands, it's important that you address it. When you let it go, it will most likely continue and could get worse. It's usually not a good idea to approach parents and fans right after a game. They are still wound up and emotional. Wait until they've had a chance to cool off so they're more willing to listen to you and to reflect on their behavior. Remind them they are role models for their child and others who are present. Also, tell them you need their help in building and maintaining an environment that promotes character. You might even have to tell some parents and fans that they won't be allowed to attend games if they continue to use foul language.

The best way to deal with this issue is through Proactive Teaching. Address the issue of inappropriate language with kids and parents at the beginning of the year to head off problems before they happen. Tell them your expectations and possible consequences, and explain that you want only positive and encouraging messages from everyone. In the end, the most effective way to let players, parents, and fans know your language expectations is by modeling and meeting them yourself.

Use Proper Conduct with Players, Opponents, and Officials

Coaches spend a lot of time talking to their players about the importance of staying focused and composed when adversity strikes. But at the first sign of trouble – a player's mistake or a perceived poor call by an official – some coaches "lose it." They begin yelling at and criticizing those around them, creating a negative and hostile atmosphere filled with blame and excuses. No one wants to be part of that, especially young people who participate to have fun and learn from supportive and caring adults.

In youth sports, everyone involved is usually fairly new to their roles and responsibilities, so kids and adults will make mistakes. Players are learning new skills and they'll make mistakes – both physical and behavioral. Opponents, parents, and fans will behave in ways that make you shake your head in disbelief or become frustrated and upset. Officials are usually novices who are trying the best they can, and they'll get some calls right and some wrong. You'll also make your share of mistakes as a coach. The key here is to understand and accept all this going in. When you are prepared ahead of time, it takes the sting out of the inevitable mistakes, misbehavior, and problems that pop up. This helps you to respond in a positive, appropriate, and constructive manner.

We define proper conduct as using behaviors and skills that foster and build respect for all those involved. This starts with how you respond to situations and treat others. Most of the time, you have no control over the mistakes others make. But you do have control over your own behavior and how you respond. So it's important for you to stay composed and positive with players, parents, opponents, fans, and officials. When you fly off the handle, others will too. It's up to you to be the voice of reason and to model proper conduct for others.

Does this mean you'll never raise your voice, become emotional, or behave in ways you'd like to take back? No. There will be times when you become frustrated with players, officials, parents, or opponents. Sometimes, your emotions will get the best of you and you'll react in less-than-perfect ways. That's okay as long as it's the exception and not the rule. Remember, an important part of your job is to model for others how to remain upbeat, positive, understanding, and encouraging even when facing unpleasant events.

There are certain situations and issues that can frustrate and anger coaches. Knowing this ahead of time can help you prepare for how best to respond when they come up. Let's look at a few of these:

Player Mistakes

Constantly yelling at kids about their performance or energy level isn't an effective way to help them improve. Some youngsters simply shut down when adults become negative. Eventually, most kids will tune you out because they think whatever they do won't be good enough. The fun gets sucked out of practices and games and players complain and want to quit. It's okay to be intense with players, and you can even raise your voice to get their attention. But if you do it all the time, it loses its effectiveness. Instead, work with and correct youngsters in an open, honest, and encouraging way that shows you care. Kids respond best to this kind of positive coaching style.

Pay close attention to how you correct young people. There are lots of well-meaning coaches who have mistreated players by using a poor teaching strategy. For example, a youth football coach made a player who the coach thought was not aggressive during a game wear a girl's skirt at the next practice. (Yes, this really happened!) This is humiliating, hurtful, and wrong. And it's an irresponsible action that could harm a child. The best way this coach could have handled this situation would have been to talk to the whole team about being more aggressive and not singling out one player for ridicule. Then the coach could have worked with players in practice to teach what he wanted.

A good tool for keeping track of players' behavioral and physical progress is a "Team Notebook." (You can use any kind of bound notebook for this.) Following each practice and game, write down the positive and negative things that happened with players. This includes behavior, character, and performance issues. For example, if a player struggles with accepting your coaching, write down the situation, skill name, what you taught the child, any consequences you gave, and how the youth responded.

This tool benefits you in a couple of ways. It helps you track progress kids are making with positive and negative behavior, character, and performance patterns. If you know whether a child is improving or struggling, you can develop a teaching plan to meet the child's individual needs. It also gives you something on paper you can show a disgruntled parent who complains to you about something like his or her child's playing time. Having this information at your fingertips allows you to confidently and professionally tell parents the exact reasons why a player is in a certain position or why he or she earned a specific consequence. It's an invaluable "reminder" tool because kids forget about their past misbehavior and parents don't see what's going on behind the scenes in practice.

Officials' Calls

Too many coaches and parents yell at or criticize officials during and after games. Blaming officials for poor performances or losses should be strictly off limits in youth sports. They aren't professionals; they're doing the best they can to get things right. Give them the benefit of the doubt. When you blame officials, all you do is give kids a crutch or an excuse for not doing their best and teach them not to take ownership of their actions and performance.

The fact is, officials rarely have a hand in a game's outcome. Tell your players this and teach them to keep focused on things they can control. Show players and parents how to respect officials by setting a good example. Shake hands with officials before games and wish them luck. During games, compliment them on the calls they get right instead of constantly yelling and criticizing. Also, engage in some lighthearted banter or talk during breaks in the game; after all it's just a game, not life or death. After the game, shake hands again and thank them for a job well done. In the post-game huddle, tell your players the officials did a good job or the best they could.

When you promote and model these kinds of positive actions toward officials on a consistent basis, kids and fans will too.

Opponent and Fan Conduct

No issue is so big or important that coaches need to scream at or confront opponents or fans. You might come across an opponent who plays dirty or bends the rules to gain an unfair advantage, or fans who are unruly and yell negative things at you and your players. When this happens, it's important for you to keep your head and not allow your emotions to take over. To prepare for these kinds of situations, go through possible scenarios and decide how you will react and conduct yourself. This kind of preparation is just as important as any game plan.

It's not a good idea to try to solve problems you experience with opponents, fans, or parents right after an incident or a game. If you or parents and fans who come to you to complain are upset, it's best to give everyone some time and space to cool down. Be honest with others and calmly tell them you want to give them and the problem your full time and attention. Also tell them that hashing it out right there and then isn't going to be productive. Tell them you want to work toward a positive solution in a cooperative and reasonable way that satisfies everyone, and that the best way to do this is to meet at a later date. Many times, you'll find that the issue gets dropped because people have time to reflect and decide the matter isn't a big deal. If you have to meet, be prepared to lay out a plan of action for how to address the issue.

Your conduct as a coach shouldn't be much different than your conduct in the workplace. If your behavior is unacceptable at work, it's probably unacceptable at practices and games, too. Pay attention to your dress, language, and conduct at all times. The best way to promote and build a fun, caring, and supportive atmosphere is to be professional and show kids and parents through your actions how to conduct themselves. If you are patient, respectful, and positive, others will be too.

COMMUNICATE WITH PARENTS

Successfully teaching young people character skills requires a team effort. Coaches and parents must work together to make the youth sports experience as productive and fun as possible. It's difficult to accomplish your teaching goals and tasks when you are at odds with parents. You need their support. This is why it's so important for you to build and maintain positive relationships with parents. One of the best ways to do this is through good and consistent communication.

Today, families are busier than ever. They have commitments to work, school, church, family, extracurricular activities, and more. Youth sports are just one of many commitments on a family's calendar. It takes a great deal of time and effort for parents to plan a schedule where everyone manages to meet their obligations. The last thing parents need is a youth coach who is unorganized and always throwing a bunch of surprises their way.

Like most things in life, youth sports will have its share of unexpected problems and last-minute changes. Most parents understand and accept this as long as it's not the norm and you communicate news to them right away. When you keep them up to speed on issues with their child, practice and game schedule changes, and other things that pop up, parents will be more supportive of you and more confident in your abilities. But the opposite is also true. When you communicate poorly, parents will grow frustrated, be less supportive, and lose confidence in you and your ability to get the job done.

Let Parents Know Your Rules and Expectations Ahead of Time

Many parents, especially those new to youth sports, have a preconceived idea of what the experience will be like for them and their child. Lots of times this view is out of sync with what will actually take place. For example, some parents might think their child should play only a certain position or that winning is the most important thing. However, you might believe it's best for youngsters to learn how to play every position and that learning skills, having fun, and other factors take precedence over winning. That's why it's important for you to communicate your coaching philosophy to parents and players and how it affects these kinds of issues.

The first step is to hold a mandatory meeting for parents and players before your first practice. Here, you can describe and discuss your coaching philosophy, behavior and performance expectations, and practice and game schedules. Also, let parents and players know how you will run practices and games. This gives everyone an opportunity to ask questions and work through any issues they might have about how and why you do certain things. This meeting puts everyone on the same page and helps you begin building a positive relationship with parents.

I held one of these meetings the year I coached my son's flag football team. Just before the season started, I called all the players and parents together. First, I asked the kids to face their parents and thank them for allowing them to play on the team and for taking them to and from practices and games. The parents were surprised but pleased by this request. Next, I talked about my expectations for players, parents, and fans, practice and game schedules, and my contact information. The parents left the meeting with a good first impression. They knew how I operated and were fully informed about what to expect. I continued to stress good communication throughout the season, and we had a fun and successful year that was free of any major problems with parents.

There are so many ways to communicate with people today – meetings, email, phone, handouts, etc. – that there's really no excuse for poor communication or failing to keep every parent informed. If parents are unable to make the pre-season parent-player meeting, there are many other ways to let them know what was covered. You could make a phone call, send an email, or mail a handout that contains the meeting information. These same lines of communication can be used throughout the year for other updates. Pick the ones that work best for you and the majority of parents. And be prepared to be flexible and patient. Even when you do your job to keep parents informed, some of them may not always respond or return the favor.

Notify Parents of Changes or Concerns

If you regularly inform parents about schedule changes at the last minute, you'll have problems. Parents will grow disgruntled and frustrated and players will miss practices and games due to conflicts. To avoid all this, notify parents as soon as you become aware of any changes in times or locations for practice or games so they have plenty of time to adjust their schedule.

As for concerns, tell parents about any behavior or performance issue you might have with their child. This way, you can enlist their help. Sometimes, all it takes is a parent's backing and some additional teaching at home to help solve a problem. It's just as important to inform parents when their child is doing well. If a player is upbeat, positive, and consistently uses character skills correctly, reinforce the behavior by telling his or her parents! It's fun to be the bearer of good news, and players and parents appreciate it.

Also, notify parents about changes you are considering in a child's playing time. This can be a volatile issue with some parents. Some are concerned only about how much their child plays and they don't care about much else. You might decide to reduce a youngster's playing time because of performance or behavior issues at practice or because you're trying something new for the next game. Whatever the reason, you can head off trouble by taking a few minutes after practice or before a game to let parents know what's going on.

Be Empathetic

Always remember that you are working with a parent's most precious gift – his or her child. Be just as understanding, patient, and kind with parents as you are with their kids. When you talk with parents about their child, do it in a way that's positive and helpful and not insensitive or hurtful. The last thing you want to do is damage your relationship with parents.

For example, if a child is having problems following instructions during practice, don't tell her parent: *"Jamie just doesn't do what I tell her and I'm getting tired of it!"* This statement offers nothing productive, is too vague, and doesn't let parents know how they can help. All you're really doing is complaining. Also, the parent could become defensive and you could lose a valuable ally.

Instead, make a statement that has substance and deliver it in a calm, positive way. You might say something like, *"Jamie's a great kid and I enjoy coaching her. Lately, she's struggled with following instructions during practices. She's earned consequences the last two practices and today she had to sit out of the scrimmage for ten minutes. I really want to nip this in the bud, and I'd appreciate it if you could talk to her about focusing more on following instructions during practice."* Here, you're telling parents exactly what's going on and how they can help, and you're doing it in an empathetic, understanding, and kind manner. When you use this approach, parents are more likely to respond favorably and be willing to help.

Communicating with parents is a necessary and important part of coaching. Good coaches do it well by telling parents the rules and expectations upfront, relaying schedule changes in a timely manner, and passing on information about positive and negative player issues as they come up. Good communication also involves using empathy and saying things in a way that helps draw a positive response from parents. When you communicate well and keep parents up to date, you create a healthy partnership that can help you meet your goals with kids.

UNDERSTAND THE BIG PICTURE

Many of today's youth sports organizations require kids and their parents to make commitments that are more in line with those expected of high school and even college athletes. To participate on "elite" or "select" teams, youngsters and parents must agree to travel to out-of-state games and tournaments; purchase uniforms, team gear, and equipment; take part in year-round training sessions; and do extensive fundraising. All this can be very expensive and time consuming for kids, parents, and coaches. With so much invested, it's easy for adults to lose sight of the big picture of making sure the kids have fun and learn and instead become fixated only on competition and winning.

That's not to say competition and winning aren't important. Success in athletics does involve coaches and players being competitive and having a desire to win. And everyone gets satisfaction out of playing hard and achieving victory. But good youth coaches don't make these the main goals of sports. When you allow yourself, your players, and parents to become hyper-competitive and focus solely on winning, the big picture becomes a very small picture. This only creates pressure and stress that can undermine the positive impact sports can have on kids' lives.

Understanding the big picture means having coaches who keep youth sports in the proper perspective and help others do the same. This means adjusting goals to match the kids' goals of having fun, spending time with friends, getting fit, learning new skills, and being part of a team. The last thing you want to do is create and foster an atmosphere where young players are expected to behave and perform like mini-professional athletes. It's much more important to cultivate an environment where everyone views youth sports in a positive light, one where youngsters are allowed to be part-time athletes and full-time kids.

Teach Life Skills Through Sports

One way to keep youth sports in the proper perspective is to put teaching character skills and life lessons at the top of your goal list. This means making it a priority to blend specific skills and lessons into your everyday instruction. Teaching players skills like being on time, listening, accepting criticism, and following instructions will do more to help them succeed in life than hours of drills on how to hit, kick, or throw a ball.

Like most young coaches, I didn't always think this was true. When I first started, I thought good coaching was all about being proficient at the "X's and O's" – devising strategies and putting together winning game plans. Over the years, my coaching philosophy has changed. Today, it's really very simple: "To use the game of football to build a better young man." Athletics are a way to help prepare young people for life. The character skills and life lessons learned on the practice field and during games are what matter most and what will have the greatest impact on young people's lives.

Almost all situations in sports – good and bad, wins and losses – are opportunities to teach kids skills and life lessons. One of your coaching responsibilities is to help youngsters learn from their sports experiences. This is especially true during the times a player or the team is struggling.

Overcoming adversity is an inevitable part of life; it's also part of the very fabric of the sporting experience. One of the greatest gifts you can give youngsters is teaching them how to bounce back from adversity, and athletics is a great training ground for practicing and learning how to do this. Kids can then take what they've learned and apply it to other situations in their life. When you use sports to prepare young people and give them the necessary skills and tools for getting back up when they've been knocked down, you're certainly respecting and focusing on the big picture.

Emphasize Competing, Not Defeating

In sports, there are certain things you can control and others you can't. So it makes sense that you should spend most of your time working with players on the two areas they have control over: preparation and effort. It's important that you get players ready for games by developing good practice plans, working with them and the team in practice to improve, and devising a game-day strategy. You also must motivate and teach your players how to give maximum effort so they can play their best. When you do these things, you set up your players and team for opportunities to achieve good performance and success.

This means not worrying or thinking about all the things that are beyond your control, like how your opponents and their fans will behave, how your opponents will play, or how the officials will call a game. What many youth coaches don't realize is that winning and losing also fall into this category.

Many variables can influence the outcome of a game – a bad bounce, lousy weather, a sick player, poor court or field conditions, and many others. That's why there's no benefit to spending time talking with your players about winning and losing. Always keep your focus on their preparation and effort. When players do these two things well, the team has a much better chance to succeed and it's easier for you, your players, and fans to accept the outcome.

Win or lose, it's important for coaches to keep their composure. Never get too elated about a win or too deflated about a loss. Take the good with the bad, and find a healthy balance between your positive and negative emotions. This is a great way to help kids and parents keep a game's outcome in the proper perspective. As long as your players have prepared well and given a good effort, you and their parents can be proud of them.

Have Fun

Why do most adults take on the awesome task of coaching boys and girls in sports? Because they enjoy it. Because they have a passion for athletic competition. Because it's FUN! Having fun and being passionate are great qualities for coaches to possess. But when coaches start taking sports too seriously, the experience can stop being fun and enjoyable for them and the kids.

Fun is the number one reason youngsters choose to play youth sports. When it stops being fun and they don't enjoy their time in athletics, they stop playing. Remember that participating in athletics is just a small part of a kid's life, not his or her entire life.

Keep practices relaxed by laughing and joking with your players. This can be a balancing act with some kids, especially at the start of the year when you're just getting to know them. Make sure you keep any joking appropriate; don't let it get out of hand, become teasing that upsets players, or let it interfere with what you're trying to accomplish at practice. Use good judgment; teach kids when it's okay to joke around and when it's time to get down to business and learn.

Toward the end of practices, use special drills, contests, or races that let players have fun and leave with smiles on their faces. After games, provide treats or ask parents to provide them. During the season, have a pizza party with players and parents to help build team unity and give you a chance to get to know everyone a bit better.

Enlist parents' help with all this. Ask them to come up with ideas for and organize fun, team-building activities and events. Getting parents involved in this way gives them a chance to join in the fun, and helps them stay positive and focused on the big picture.

The majority of your players will have other obligations, priorities, and interests they consider to be more important than sports. So don't expect them to always share the same kind of strong desire and commitment you have. Successful youth coaches understand and accept this, and work to help youngsters find a good balance between athletics and other important areas in their lives. Focus on teaching youngsters character skills and life lessons through their sports experiences, preparing and giving a good effort (instead of winning and losing), and, most importantly, keeping the athletic experience fun. When you do, you, the players, and parents can keep the big picture in view.

Summary

There are many well-intentioned youth coaches out there doing their best to provide a positive sports experience for young people. Usually, these coaches arrive on the scene with little or no training. When they try to educate themselves, they spend most of their time studying the more technical aspects of coaching: practice drills, strategy, game planning, etc. These are valuable, but they're really just a small part of what it takes to be a good and effective youth coach.

This chapter discussed eight skills that every youth coach should master and carry in his or her coaching toolbox. These skills – the things to do and ways to act – help you set and maintain the right priorities. When you teach skills, use praise and compliments, appropriately correct misbehavior, are organized, have high energy, model positive behavior, communicate with parents, and understand the big picture, you possess the keys to creating a fun, healthy, and successful sports experience for kids and adults.

PARENTING FOR CHARACTER

It seems as though many parents (myself included!) are "professional" spectators these days. There are school plays, music and dance recitals, art exhibits, youth group performances at church, and many other extracurricular activities that fill up your evenings and weekends. You go because you love your child and want to be encouraging and supportive. You also want to let your child know that what he or she is doing has value and is important. This good parenting motivates girls and boys to continue working hard toward their goals and success.

Parents need to bring this same kind of attitude, mindset, and behavior to youth sports. Your child looks to you for support and guidance, and you can either make your child's sports experience a positive and healthy one or one that's negative and harmful. When parents choose to use positive behaviors and do the right things, like praise and compliment instead of criticize, support the coaches, express concerns appropriately, and use appropriate behavior during games, they enhance the experience for everyone – their child, other players, coaches, officials, other parents, and fans.

Parents of young athletes have a tremendous influence on the atmosphere surrounding their child's sports setting. The most important task and responsibility parents have is to help create a fun and productive learning environment. It's remarkable what a detrimental effect even one parent's bad behavior can have on everyone else. One bad apple can truly spoil things for so many.

Bad behavior by parents – yelling instructions at kids during games, screaming at officials, complaining about the coaches, criticizing players' performances, and focusing solely on winning and losing – can suck the fun and life right out of athletics for all involved. Young people get embarrassed and upset, coaches grow frustrated, and other adults become annoyed and angry. Do you want to be that obnoxious parent? Do you want your bad behavior to drive a wedge into your relationship with your child, his or her coaches, other players, and their parents – all because of a game?

When it's put this way, the vast majority of parents would emphatically answer, "No!" They would much rather be the positive person who encourages and supports the players and coaches. But this can be hard to do sometimes because sports and competition involve and evoke emotions, both positive and negative ones. This isn't a bad thing; emotions are part of the very fabric of athletics and a reason why people of all ages enjoy and are attracted to competition and sports. We love getting excited and pumped up over a good game or a good match, especially when our children are playing. Emotions are a problem only when you allow them to get the best of you and express them in negative and harmful ways.

This is more likely to happen when you have unrealistic expectations riding on your child's and the team's performance. When parents zero in on the wrong outcomes, like winning championships and trophies, snagging college scholarships, and playing professionally, they are going to be disappointed much more often than they are satisfied. It's important for parents to be realistic about their expectations and goals for youngsters who participate in athletics. The focus always needs to be on what kids want from the experience, not what parents expect.

It's also important for parents to change their behavior and become better role models for how to react and behave in youth athletics. This can be difficult for many parents because they're not sure what to do or because they've become "locked in" to behaving in ways that are disruptive and negative. This is where the *Competing with Character* parent skills come in. They provide you with the roadmap to becoming a positive role model, and can help you learn how to constructively deal with situations that often cause parents problems.

The decision is up to you. Do you want to be a positive force in your child's athletic setting? Do you want your son or daughter to get the most out of his or her athletic experience? If your answer is "Yes," then read on!

105

You'll learn what it takes to be part of the solution instead of the problem. One of the best gifts you can give your child is letting the youth sports experience be his or hers and not yours.

In this chapter, we'll review and discuss seven youth sports skills for parents. Learning these skills is not enough; you also have to use them, everywhere, all the time. When you do, you'll be in a great position to help coaches and other parents create and maintain a setting that promotes and teaches youngsters all the positive character skills and life lessons that can come with playing sports.

SKILLS FOR PARENTS AND TIPS FOR SUCCESS

1. Have Your Child Be on Time with Proper Equipment

- Write it down.
- Help your child share the responsibility.
- Notify coaches if there is a problem.

2. Support the Coaches

- Avoid negative talk.
- Ask if there is anything you can do.
- Tell them thanks.

3. Voice Concerns Appropriately

- Avoid talking to coaches right after a game or competition.
- Remain calm and use an appropriate voice tone.
- State your concerns, listen, and have an open mind.

4. Praise and Compliment Your Child Rather than Criticize

- Look for the positives.
- Praise three times for every correction or criticism (3-to-1 Rule).
- Make connections between appropriate behavior and desired outcomes.

5. Model Appropriate Behavior at Athletic Contests

- Cheer for your team, not against your opponents.
- Respect all game officials.
- Don't criticize, be positive.

6. Emphasize Effort and Enjoyment over Winning

- Avoid conversations about "how many" or "how much."
- Don't draw comparisons between your child and other kids.
- Praise kids for their efforts immediately after contests, win or lose.

7. Problem-Solve Issues Your Child Has with Coaches

- Stay neutral and avoid making negative comments about the coach.
- Practice with your child how to advocate for himself or herself with the coach.
- Support the coaches' right to make decisions.

HAVE YOUR CHILD BE ON TIME WITH PROPER EQUIPMENT

This is one area where coaches need your help. They can organize and distribute practice and game schedules and draw up great practice plans, but they don't mean much if kids always arrive late and unprepared. You can be a huge help to coaches by making sure your child gets to practice and games on time with everything he or she needs. When one player is late or doesn't have his glove or helmet or her kneepads or shoes, everyone is affected. The practice plan a coach labored over might have to be scrapped or adjusted on the fly because there are not enough players to properly run a drill or activity, or a youngster who plays a specific position is missing. Other players who are on time are forced to wait around for the tardy player and miss the benefits of a full practice. And when practices run late because they start late, it throws off pick-up schedules for parents.

Being punctual and prepared lets coaches know that you and your child respect, value, and appreciate their time. This skill also plays an important role in almost every aspect of a child's life (school, work, etc.). Young people learn that they must follow through with their individual responsibilities if the team or group is to succeed. Finally, the skill helps set the tone for a practice. Everyone is on the same page and working together to learn and get better.

Being on time also means picking up your child when practice is over. Most youth sports coaches are volunteering their time and have other responsibilities. Part of a coach's job is to stay at the practice or game site until all the players are picked up by a parent or someone else who is responsible for them. Coaches won't leave a youngster unattended to wait for his or her ride, but they aren't supposed to be babysitters. In addition, kids, especially younger ones, can become anxious and frightened when their ride is late. To avoid these kinds of problems, make it a priority to be punctual!

Write It Down

Once your child gets his or her practice and game schedules, get a calendar and make it your sports or activity planner. Write in all the practice and game times, their locations, and any other information that might be needed. Make it the gathering place for all your sports information. Put the calendar on your refrigerator or somewhere everyone, including your child, can see it. In addition, help your child make a list of required equipment. Use this as a checklist when it's time for your child to head to practices and games. Post the list next to your sports calendar for easy reference. Doing these two simple things teaches your child how to be organized and prepared.

Help Your Child Share the Responsibility

When you create your sports calendar and equipment checklist, make sure your child helps. If he or she is old enough, have your child write down everything. You can check the information to make sure it's accurate. Then put your child in charge of the calendar and equipment checklist. Tell your child he or she is responsible for keeping the calendar and list updated and for telling you about upcoming practices and games. Obviously, you'll know the schedule, but this helps your child learn how to get ready without you having to constantly remind him or her. Kids need to be aware too; that's how they learn to be organized and responsible.

Notify Coaches If There Is a Problem

Coaches understand that players will sometimes be late for or miss a practice or game. Conflicts and emergencies come up from time to time. The best way for you to handle this is to notify the coach right away. This gives him or her an opportunity to prepare or make adjustments. Also, coaches worry when a player doesn't show up and they don't know why. It's very easy for you to keep coaches informed about any issue that might affect your child and the schedule. Simply send an email or call and leave a voice message. Don't wait until the last minute; tell coaches as early as possible about any scheduling issue.

Support the Coaches

SKILL

The vast majority of youth coaches are involved in athletics because they enjoy working with and being around young people. They certainly aren't in it for the money. Most are unpaid volunteers, not professionals; they simply have a love for sports and are willing to share their time and experience with your kids.

Coaches usually come into the game knowing that players will make mistakes and cause some problems. They also understand that a child or two might get upset and even throw a tantrum. This comes with the coaching territory. However, what youth coaches don't expect or need are parents who act like their kids.

Coaches need parents to act like adults and work out problems and misunderstandings in mature and productive ways. Always keep in mind that youth coaches will make mistakes just like everyone else. They're trying their best to help your child have a positive experience. It's important for you to be encouraging and give them the benefit of the doubt. When parents and coaches work together, everyone can have a great experience.

What coaches want most from you is support. They need you to help out where needed and they feel rewarded when you show appreciation. Just like with your kids, you can make the difference in whether a coach's experience is enjoyable or miserable.

Avoid Negative Talk

It's amazing how quickly bleacher talk can turn sour. And it only takes one person to start it. A parent might disagree with the coach's strategy, think his or her child should be playing more, or be angry because the team is losing. If the parent decides to complain to other parents, it doesn't take long for those who are also disgruntled to jump onboard. Soon, the stands are filled with an unhappy group of parents grumbling about coaches and players. Once this vicious cycle starts, it's hard to stop.

It's not only important to stay away from negative conversations, complaints, and criticism about coaches, but also to stop them when they do start. They're unproductive, unfair, and harmful to everyone involved. Sometimes, you might have to be the voice of reason that calms the waters and gets everyone back on track. When parents get themselves so worked up over what's going on, they can't possibly enjoy watching their children play. Coaches become angry and resentful because they feel undermined and unsupported. And players are embarrassed by their parents' bad behavior and baffled by why parents take a kids' game so seriously. When the bleacher talk turns negative, no one wins.

So what can you do to keep negative talk from starting or stop it once it begins? The best thing is to be proactive. From the start of the season to the end, praise coaches for all the good things they do. Make a commitment to be the positive parent who sets a positive tone by modeling supportive behavior.

When complaints and criticism sprout up around you, don't get involved. Simply stay quiet and avoid fueling the fire. If it continues, find another place to sit with parents who are upbeat and positive, or just watch alone. Many times, getting up and moving is enough to send a message to others that their behavior is out of line and should stop. There's no reason for you to stay in the middle of the negativity and allow it to ruin your experience.

At some point, you might feel the need to support your child's coaches by saying something to parents who continue to be critical. If you do, remain calm and polite, and use the *Competing with Character* parent skill of "Support the Coaches." You might say something like, *"Remember, we're supposed to be role models for the kids. Let's compete with character and avoid any negative talk about coaches. Let's be positive and encouraging."* This is a simple reminder about appropriate parent behavior. Most parents will understand and stop complaining, but some won't. When this happens, don't get involved in a debate or argument. Simply walk away and watch the game from another spot.

It's especially important for parents to avoid making negative comments about coaches around children. This can lead to some real problems. First, it lets youngsters use the coaches as an excuse for poor performance and misbehavior. Second, kids learn that it's okay to blame others and not take responsibility for themselves and their actions.

When parents say bad things about a coach, they risk damaging their child's relationship with the coach. Parents have a powerful influence over what their children think and how they act. So when parents speak about and treat coaches poorly, youngsters are likely to do the same.

You also can directly affect how youngsters view their athletic experience. When they continually hear parents bad-mouthing the coach, it casts a dark shadow over everything, including practices and games. The result is that kids are less likely to have fun.

The way to avoid these problems and help youngsters enjoy their time in athletics is to talk positively about coaches. Remind kids that coaches are giving their time freely and doing the best they can. When the inevitable mistakes happen, don't bash them. Instead, explain to your child that everyone makes mistakes and it's not a big deal. Most of all, always be on the lookout for the good things coaches do. When you're positive and supportive, the kids will be too, and they'll be much more likely to enjoy playing sports.

Ask If There Is Anything You Can Do

It's a struggle for coaches to try to do it all. It's a real challenge during the season to balance coaching youth sports with responsibilities at home and work. So youth coaches rely on parental involvement big time. Your help is crucial to creating an athletic setting that runs as smoothly and efficiently as possible.

There are many different things you can volunteer to do. You can help run drills at practice or be in charge of equipment and uniforms. During games, you can keep statistics or run the game clock or scoreboard. You can volunteer to organize fun team-building activities or bring treats and drinks to games. Some kids might need rides to practices and games, so you can help arrange a carpool schedule. Or, you can help out with administrative tasks like putting together practice and game schedules. Work with the coach to find something that fits you, your strengths, and your time.

When parents rally and take on some of these smaller but very important tasks, coaches are able to spend more time teaching and helping players improve. Also, coaches feel supported and see that parents are willing to work together as a team. When you're involved in the right way, you get to know the coach better and are more likely to have a positive relationship with him or her.

Tell Them Thanks

Most coaches aren't looking for accolades from parents and players. They're giving freely of their time because they have a passion for sports and a desire to work with young people. The greatest reward for youth coaches is the satisfaction of knowing that what they do matters and that they're having a positive impact on young peoples' lives. In order for coaches to feel like they've accomplished these things, it's important for you and other parents to express your appreciation.

After every practice and game, make it a point to tell coaches "Thanks." And make sure your child does the same. Thank coaches for their time and effort. When you see your child improve, or when he or she tells you about a positive interaction or experience with the coach, tell the coach. He or she will love to hear that the kids are enjoying themselves and learning, whether it's on or off the fields and courts. Simple gestures of gratitude from you and your child can go a long way in helping coaches feel supported and good about what they're doing.

People don't get into youth coaching for the big pay or to build a career – they just enjoy spending time teaching young people how to play a sport. There aren't a lot of external rewards for youth coaches. One reward parents can give them is support. You can do this by staying positive in the bleachers and when talking about coaches with your child and other parents, helping where needed, and thanking coaches for all they do.

Voice Concerns Appropriately

At some time while your child participates in youth sports, a concern or issue will come up that you'll want to talk over with a coach. It might be about your child's playing time, performance, or behavior. Or, you might need to discuss practice and game schedules, equipment, or travel plans, or make the coach aware of a medical (asthma), medication (insulin for a diabetic), or mental health (anxiety, shyness, etc.) issue.

When discussing these matters with coaches, your goal should always be to work with them as a team to arrive at a solution that's best for and satisfies you, your child, and the coach. Approach any conversation with coaches in a cooperative, respectful, and pleasant manner. You want your child to get all the benefits your coaches can provide; how you go about delivering your message is key to ensuring that that happens.

Most coaches understand the emotional invest-ment you have in your child. There may be times when your emotions get the best of you and you do and say things you regret. When this happens, you risk alienating the very person you need to help your child succeed in athletics. Emotions become a problem when they get in the way of your ability to work together with others. The parent skill and tips for success presented in this section can help you stay level-headed and team up with coaches to arrive at effective solutions.

Remember that youth coaches are trying to balance your child's needs with those of the team and other play-ers. This is always a challenge. The best way you can help is to recognize that it's not all about your child, that there are other youngsters and parents who also require the coach's time and attention. Coaches will do their best to listen and provide what parents ask of them, but you have to be open and willing to cooperate and compromise.

If you think something needs to be brought to the coach's attention, feel free to do it. Follow your con-science and use good judgment. And don't allow some-thing to sit and fester for too long. If a concern or issue really bothers you, the best thing to do is get it out in the open. But, make sure you're prepared to do it in a pro-ductive and positive way. The *Competing with Character* parent skill for voicing concerns appropriately will help you do just that.

Avoid Talking to Coaches Right after a Game or Competition

After a Boys Town football game a couple of years ago, I was dissatisfied with the players' effort and performance. Even though we won, I felt they didn't play up to their abilities as individuals or as a team. In the locker room following the game, I was upset and proceeded to read them the riot act. The next day, I watched film of the game and saw that our players *did* work hard and did many more things right than wrong. Immediately, I regretted not taking time to cool down and gather my thoughts before I spoke. At the next practice, I apologized to the players and praised them for the good things they had done in the game.

The emotions of coaches, players, parents, and fans tend to run high after games. This is especially true when the team loses. Unfortunately, some parents think this is a good time to complain to coaches about playing time or criticize their game decisions and strategy. Their negative emotions usually cloud their thinking and they react in inappropriate and potentially harmful ways.

Parents should refrain from having discussions with coaches immediately after games or competitions. In fact, it's best to wait a day or two before bringing a concern or issue to a coach (unless it's an emergency). When parents take time to gather their thoughts and get their emotions under control, they're better able to decide if they even need to talk to the coach. Many times, they'll realize that their concern grew out of the heat of the moment and isn't worth pursuing. Time gives everyone a better perspective on things, and you can rarely go wrong when you're reflective and patient.

If you find yourself in this situation, and, after a cool-down period, still feel you need to talk with a coach, then do so. Contact him or her to set up a time and place for the discussion. You might decide to talk on the phone or meet in person before or after a practice. Allow time to pass so you can determine whether the issue is truly important and for you and the coach to be composed and ready to work together.

Remain Calm and Use an Appropriate Voice Tone

A conversation can quickly escalate into a misunderstanding or an argument when one person raises his or her voice and loses composure. The other person usually becomes defensive and unwilling to listen because he or she feels threatened and challenged. When a parent comes to a coach angry and accusatory, the parent is probably going to get tuned out and be disappointed with the results.

The only behaviors you can control are your own. If you have to talk with your child's coaches and you want them to listen and respond favorably, then it's up to you to set the right tone. This means being calm, cool, and collected, and using an even, conversational voice tone from the beginning of the discussion to the end.

Coaches are more willing to work together with parents when they are approached in a mature and cooperative manner. No one wins when a discussion becomes a test of wills or the participants become fixated on who's right and who's wrong. Instead, parents and coaches should work on creating an atmosphere of openness, trust, and teamwork by beginning conversations only when everyone is prepared and composed.

State Your Concerns, Listen, and Have an Open Mind

When you meet with a coach, state your concern in a straightforward and nonjudgmental manner, and stick to the facts. Avoid saying something like, *"Jane hardly plays anymore. She says you don't like her and have it in for her. Why are you being so unfair?"* Presenting a concern like this will get you nowhere. Immediately, the coach is put on the defensive. There is no invitation for a real conversation; you've already reached a conclusion and are demanding an explanation.

A better way to handle this would be to say something like, *"Jane's played less than she normally does the last two games. Is there a problem or something I should be aware of?"* Here, you're inviting a dialogue and requesting help in gathering the facts. With this approach, you're much more likely to get a full and accurate account of the situation, along with a solution you can live with.

Once you state your concern, it's important to listen to the coach's response. Parents don't always know what's going on behind the scenes in practice, and your child might not be telling you the whole story. The purpose of your conversation with the coach is to get a true picture of what's going on so you can work toward a positive solution.

In the previous example, your child might have told you the coach is being unfair for no good reason. However, when you talk with the coach, he or she might tell you there have been behavior problems at practice or that your child hasn't been giving much effort. There are almost always logical explanations for why kids earn consequences from coaches. It's up to you not to rush to judgment and to listen to all sides.

Keep an open mind when talking to coaches about a concern or issue. Don't go into the conversation thinking "not my child." Let's face it, kids tend to exaggerate, don't always tell the truth, and may not be able to correctly interpret, understand, or relay the true nature of a situation. You're usually not going to get a completely accurate assessment of what's going on from your child. Sometimes, he or she won't even be close! This is why parents need to seek the input and counsel of coaches. They're adults, and they will give you a much more reliable and precise report. Real problems result when parents blindly and automatically believe their child's version without ever consulting the coach. Be sure to thoroughly and patiently seek input from all sides before arriving at any conclusions.

Once you've gathered all the facts from everyone, work with the coach to arrive at a satisfactory solution. Many times, this will involve compromise on your part. Ultimately, the coach is in charge of the athletic setting, so be prepared to accept a decision that isn't exactly what you want. When this happens, use it as a teaching opportunity for your child. Explain that the coach is an authority figure, much like a teacher at school or a boss at work and that, sometimes, you have to live with his or her final decision. When you're done talking with coaches, thank them for their time and effort.

Finally, if after all this, you still aren't satisfied with the outcome, tell the coach you'd like to discuss the matter with another authority figure in the athletic setting, like an athletic director or the director of the youth sports organization. As always, do this calmly and in an appropriate manner. Sometimes, a third party can help when emotions are running too high or the situation is deteriorating. Be selective about what you decide to bring to a third party. The majority of the time, these authority figures will defer to and support their coaches, especially when it involves issues like playing time, lineups, game strategy, and other issues that have to do with coaching decisions. They will let their coaches coach and get involved only when necessary.

It's a sure bet that problems, issues, and concerns will arise as your child enjoys youth sports. It's up to parents to approach and handle these situations with maturity and composure. The goal is to work together with coaches to arrive at a fair solution for all involved. Parents can do this by allowing time to pass before talking to coaches, staying calm, and being willing to compromise.

4 SKILL · PRAISE AND COMPLIMENT YOUR CHILD RATHER THAN CRITICIZE

Many parents have extremely high and, sometimes, unrealistic expectations for their kids and their kids' coaches when it comes to youth sports. The stakes become dangerously high when parents anticipate and even demand perfect performances, overwhelming victories, and championship seasons. This magnifies mistakes and poor performances, creating an atmosphere filled with tension and pressure. In the name of success, parents can begin zeroing in on, pointing out, and correcting flaws rather than on catching kids being good and encouraging them to have fun.

It's important for parents to remember that players and youth coaches are novices, not experts. There will be *lots* of mistakes and much to correct. This is all part of the learning process, and players and coaches will do the best they can to improve and succeed. But when the focus is constantly on flaws, failure, and correction, everyone will quickly get discouraged, grow frustrated, and feel they can't do anything right. What they need to help get them through the tough learning curves are parents who praise, compliment, encourage, and support.

Kids want to enjoy their youth sports experience and have fun. As we've said many times, it's their number one goal and should be yours, too. It's important for parents to stop mumbling and grumbling about every little mistake, poor performance, or loss and turn their attention to catching kids and coaches doing the right things. This will go a long way toward creating the kind of pleasant and fun-filled athletic experience your child and others desire and deserve.

Look for the Positives

In their efforts to improve and succeed, players and coaches will struggle and experience disappointment and failure. They'll be trying hard, and the last thing they need is a parent piling on the criticism. So instead of being a critic, be a cheerleader – someone who finds the good in the bad, inspires others to give their best, and motivates players and coaches to keep moving forward.

Let's face it, the negative, pessimistic parent just brings everyone down; no one really wants to be around him or her. But parents who focus on the positive are uplifting and great to be around. Through their attitude, words, and actions, they take the pressure off players and coaches to perform perfectly and win big, and instead cheer them on to do their best and have fun. And you can't ask anything more than that from youngsters and coaches.

Make it a priority to be the positive parent who sets the tone in the stands, during the drive home from games and practices, and at home. Look for the good things players and coaches do, no matter how small or insignificant they might seem, and tell them "Great job!" and encourage them to keep their heads up when they're down. Positive action like this is contagious and others will follow your lead.

Praise Three Times for Every Correction or Criticism (3-to-1 Rule)

We follow what we call the "3-to-1 Rule" with our players at Boys Town. This means that for every negative consequence or correction a youngster earns for inappropriate behavior, we look for at least three opportunities to praise and reinforce him or her for using a positive behavior. With some kids, especially those who get discouraged easily, the ratio can be as high as 8 to 1 or 10 to 1; it all depends on the youth and his or her individual needs.

Our motto is "Catch 'em being good!" For many adults – parents included – a positive approach like this is awkward and sometimes difficult to put into practice. Why? Because many parents simply expect youngsters to be able to do the right thing and make good choices. They believe kids should be doing these things anyway, and since it all should come naturally, why praise them?

Well, it doesn't come naturally. Kids often struggle to do the next right thing and make sound decisions. Looking for positive behaviors to praise doesn't mean you ignore negative behaviors; you still continue to address and correct them. But you're always on the lookout for the good thing kids (and coaches) do. Praising and reinforcing young people when they take the right action or make good decisions motivates them to repeat those positive behaviors and lets them know you notice when they do. Catching kids being good is one of the keys to helping kids feel confident about themselves and their ability to succeed.

Make Connections between Appropriate Behavior and Desired Outcomes

Youngsters benefit from knowing why a skill or behavior is helpful to them or others. This is called giving kids "reasons." Reasons help young people make the connection between what they say or do and the possible outcomes or results of their actions. For example, if your child is ready for practice and has all the equipment he or she needs, you can give lots of reasons for why doing this is helpful:

- *"When you're prepared and ready to go to practice, we can get there early so you have some time with your friends."*

- *"When you're prepared and on time to practice, your coach really appreciates it and so do the other players."*

- *"Great job being ready and prepared for practice! Now, we have time to stop and get you a sports drink."*

Giving kids reasons like these helps them link their behavior with consequences or outcomes. Reasons are particularly effective when they can demonstrate the benefits your child might receive, either immediately or in the future. The reasons you give should be brief, believable, individual, and kid-related.

Creating a successful athletic setting where kids can learn, grow, and have fun is an important and challenging goal for youth coaches. But they can't accomplish this by themselves; they need your help. Coaches need parents to be upbeat, positive, and encouraging, and to focus their attention on all the good things players and coaches do. It's important for you to be a cheerleader, find lots of good things to praise, and give your child reasons to use positive behavior. Doing these things allows you to be one of the positive, helpful parents who goes to bat for both coaches and kids.

Model Appropriate Behavior at Athletic Contests

SKILL Parents have more influence on their child's behavior than anyone else. Almost everything your child says and does comes directly from what you say and do. If you have a funny way of saying something, your child will likely use the same words or phrase. And, how you conduct yourself in certain places and situations usually determines how your child will act in the same place or under similar circumstances. That's why modeling is one of your most powerful teaching tools.

In youth sports, setting a good example is extremely important. How parents react to adversity, disappointment, and failure goes a long way toward shaping how their kids and the team will handle tough times. If parents yell and scream nasty comments at opponents, blame and criticize officials, and complain about coaching, guess who will do the same? When parents behave this way, they're giving their kids the green light to blame others for poor performance and teaching them it's okay to behave badly in a sports setting.

Parents must be aware of what they're saying and doing at all times during games. Also, they must understand why they're there and what their role is. Your job as a fan is to cheer on and support your child, the team, and the coaches. That's it! There's no reason for you to get involved in any other way with officials, with opposing fans, players, or coaches, or with your child, the team, or coaches. (For "Rules for Spectator Conduct," see Appendix 2.)

When you do your job well, you're showing your child and others exactly what they should do, too. This kind of real-life modeling is an extremely effective and powerful way to teach young people the right way to act. Also, when parents behave, players have less anxiety about their performance and feel less pressure to win. They're free to enjoy themselves and have fun.

Always remember that you're representing yourself, your child, your family, the team, your coaches, and your organization. That's a lot of people! How you behave can either make everybody shine or give the whole group a bad name. Is it really worth damaging peoples' names and reputations over an official's call or because your team isn't winning? No. The good news is that when you conduct yourself properly, others look to you and everyone associated with you as a positive example of how to behave in youth sports.

The following sections discuss three main areas where parents sometimes struggle to set a good example in youth sports. These might be "trigger areas" that can lead to big problems, so it's important to prepare yourself and have solutions ready.

Cheer for Your Team, Not Against Your Opponents

Have you ever wondered why some parents yell for opposing players to drop pop flies or try to distract a child at the free throw line by shouting things like "Miss it!" or "Air ball!"? This kind of negative behavior does nothing but make those parents look foolish and immature. If they'd step back and see their behavior for what it really is, they would begin to understand how inappropriate, disruptive, and harmful it is to everyone involved in the athletic contest.

Is it possible for parents to cheer *for* their team without cheering against the other team? Absolutely! And it's really pretty easy: Just focus your attention on your players and your team and steer clear of any kind of negative cheering or comments toward the opposing team. When parents cheer for opponents to make mistakes, perform poorly, or fail, they create a tense and hostile environment where emotions and tempers run high and winning and beating the other team's brains out become the sole objectives.

Parents can set an excellent example and take this character skill to the next level by acknowledging an opponents' good play and performance. There's no law against clapping for and praising a nice catch, shot, or pass by a player from either team. This can set the tone for parents and players on both sides to support and encourage all participants. This creates the type of game atmosphere that's healthy and fun for kids and adults.

Respect All Game Officials

This is another area of role modeling where many parents struggle and sometimes fail miserably. Almost every youth sports contest has its share of parents on both sides who yell and scream at officials over what they believe are wrong or missed calls. It's amazing how worked up some parents can get, especially during tight games. They can get so emotional and out of hand that they're asked to quiet down, ejected, and even banned from attending future games.

Youth sports officials have two responsibilities: to make sure both teams follow the rules and to keep order. They have no allegiance to either team and they're not concerned about who wins and loses. Their job is to keep everything as fair as possible for both teams. Because officials are a neutral party (and because they're actually on the field or court), they're in a better position to make correct calls or difficult rulings. Parents, on the other hand, are biased, are likely to perceive calls or rulings that go against their team as wrong or favoring the other team, and are in the stands or on the sidelines, away from the action. This is why parents need to stick to being fans and leave the officiating to the officials.

Youth sports officials aren't professionals. Usually, they are volunteers and, many times, they're teens or young adults. They will make mistakes, so it's unrealistic to expect perfection from them. Rarely, however, will officials affect the outcome of a game. They do their best to get things right and, during the course of a game, they make many more right calls than wrong ones.

When parents display poor modeling by blaming officials for losses or bad performances, they teach youngsters that it's okay to use what someone else does as a crutch, and to not take responsibility for their own behavior, effort, and actions. Also, when parents blame and shout their displeasure at officials during games, it distracts the players and negatively affects their performance. Kids can easily get caught up in the "blame game" instead of concentrating on what they're supposed to do.

What can you do to be a positive role model when it comes to the treatment of officials? First, make youth sports officials off limits. Simply make a commitment to keep quiet when there's a close or questionable call or a difficult ruling. The hardest thing to do is to stick with this commitment during a tight, emotional game. Let the coaches handle any problems or concerns that might arise with an official. It's not a parent's place to do this from the stands.

The best thing you can do is to be positive and encouraging. When you see players on your team get frustrated or upset over a disputed call or ruling, say something encouraging to them like "It's no big deal" or "Shake it off." Also during games, tell officials "Nice call" when they get it right. This is especially effective when the call or ruling goes against your child's team. When you do this, you'll find yourself noticing all the positive things officials do and praising them more often.

One more thing you can do: Learn the rules of your child's sport. This will make you more knowledgeable about why certain calls and rulings are made or not made. When you learn the rules, you'll be less likely to argue or get upset with officials.

Remember that being an official can be a thankless job. Someone is usually going to be frustrated or upset because a call or ruling didn't go his or her way. This is why it's important for parents and their kids to thank officials after a game. This teaches players to recognize and respect the tough and important job officials have in trying to enforce rules, keep the game fair, and maintain order.

Don't Criticize, Be Positive

"Hustle!"

"Bad pass!"

"Tuck in your elbow!"

"Throw it to Johnny!"

"Get her out of there!"

These kinds of comments are commonly heard coming from parents during youth sports contests. When parents shout out instructions, advice, criticism, or complaints, they're not only being poor role models but also disrupting the game for everyone. Players get distracted, confused, and discouraged when someone other than their coach is telling them what to do or what they just did wrong. Coaches become frustrated because they're unable to clearly communicate with players. Sometimes, parents can even contradict what coaches have told or taught the players. A parent's outbursts or constant negative comments toward players and coaches also can make other parents and fans feel uncomfortable and annoyed.

As you can see, nothing good comes from criticism during your child's games. It drains the enjoyment and fun out of youth sports for players, coaches, and other parents. Competing in an athletic contest is hard enough for youngsters and youth coaches. The last thing they need is a bunch of critics in the stands. What they really need are cheerleaders! That's your job and the job of every parent.

It's not always easy being a cheerleader and staying positive – or even silent – during games, especially when they're close or things aren't going your team's way. However, this is when it's most important for you to be a good role model, keeping your emotions in check and staying upbeat and supportive. Don't allow yourself to get caught up in the heat of the moment and say things you might regret or that might embarrass your child, the team, the coaches, and you. Keep youth sports in the proper perspective by reminding yourself and others that it's just a game. Just let players play and coaches coach.

If you do find yourself getting emotional or upset, take some time to cool down. Take a few deep breaths, talk with another parent about something other than the game, or call a friend. Or, leave for a while – take a short walk, get something to drink, or take a restroom break. What you're doing here is getting your mind off the game so you can calm down. Once you've gathered yourself, you can come back refreshed and with a more positive attitude and realistic outlook.

Setting a positive example is one of the most important and effective ways parents can teach their kids how to conduct themselves during youth sports contests. Parents should be cheerleaders – and nothing else – for their child and his or her team during a match or game. This means cheering for your team and not against the opponents, respecting officials, and not criticizing players and coaches. When you follow through on these behaviors, you can be a tremendous influence on your child and those around you. Take on the challenge to change your youth sports environment. Make it your job to help fill the stands with cheerleaders who are upbeat and who encourage players and coaches to do their best.

EMPHASIZE EFFORT AND ENJOYMENT OVER WINNING

In today's world, it's easy for parents to get caught up in the hype of winning and wanting their child to be the best – and this isn't limited to just youth sports. There's competition among parents to have the best student, musician, Boy Scout, Girl Scout, dancer, artist, etc. It's not enough for young people to just participate in these activities or even to be pretty good at them – it's about standing out from the pack and being exceptional.

These kinds of expectations are unrealistic for the vast majority of kids involved in any activity, including athletics. Youngsters want to please their parents, and they'll work hard to win their approval. But kids are set up to fail when parents' expectations are out of reach. The pressure to meet them often becomes intense and overwhelming. Over time, youngsters grow discouraged and disillusioned, and any enjoyment or fun they get out of playing withers away. In the end, the sport becomes a burden and kids stop playing.

Unrealistic parental expectations can be the death of youth sports for young people. That's why it's important for you to examine your expectations, determine if they're appropriate and realistic, and decide if they mesh with and match what your child wants. Many parents come into youth sports anticipating that their child will be an "all-star" and that his or her team will win, big and often. In fact, these expectations top most parents' lists. The problem is that they're at the bottom of kids' lists.

So why are parents so obsessed with winning and having their child be the best and the brightest when their child could care less? It's a good, fair question every parent should give a lot of thought to. We know kids get involved in youth sports because they want to have fun, be with friends, stay fit, learn new skills, and be part of a team. These are good and honorable reasons to participate in any extracurricular activity. They should be good enough for adults, who must realize it doesn't have to be all about winning and being number one.

Sure, it's important for players to work hard and strive to win. But it's not the sole measuring stick for success. The ultimate gauge of a successful youth sports experience is whether a child wants to play again. If he or she does, you can be certain that the major reason is because the youngster had fun. To support that, parents should emphasize effort and enjoyment over winning.

Before we discuss the three tips for success, let's review one big way parents can take the pressure off their kids: Make practice a "parent-free zone."

It used to be that parents only went to their children's games. Today, more and more parents attend practices too. Many parents use this opportunity to overscrutinize their kids' performance and tally their mistakes as if they were keeping score at a game. Then, the ride home becomes a "coaching" session where the parent recites all the things the child needs to fix or change. Most kids can't wait to get home so they can go to their room and be alone.

The behavior of most "practice parents" defeats the very purpose of practice. Practice should be a time when boys and girls have the opportunity to learn new skills and make mistakes without the pressure and anxiety of letting their parents down. Mistakes and failure are a natural part of the learning process. Rarely will a child know naturally the best way to shoot a basketball, swing a baseball bat, or kick a soccer ball. It takes lots of time, repetitions, errors, and teaching from coaches on these physical skills in practice before kids can do them correctly and competently.

A coach's job is to guide and instruct young people through a learning process in athletics. Good coaches create an environment where players feel comfortable making mistakes and failing. They want youngsters to feel at ease and be willing to try new things, take risks, and get out of their comfort zones. This kind of positive, supportive setting allows for better and more effective teaching and learning.

When parents watch and analyze every move at practice, many youth coaches (especially new and inexperienced ones) grow tense and uneasy, which can negatively affect and influence their teaching and interactions with players. Also, kids feel pressured to perform well because they aren't comfortable making mistakes or failing in front of their parents. That's why we recommend making practices a "parent-free zone." This means parents voluntarily choose not to attend practices, unless there's a good reason. When parents leave players and coaches alone, the players and coaches can comfortably and naturally work together without any outside distractions, interference, or pressure.

There might be times when it's a good idea for you to stay for a practice. For example, your child might be having behavior problems, troubles with another player, or problems with the coach. When issues like these come up, the best thing to do is to first talk with coaches. Tell them about your concern or issue and get their input and observations. If you still think it's necessary, ask coaches if they mind you staying to watch practice so you can gather more information. During that time, just be a quiet observer and avoid calling attention to yourself. Simply do your best to let practice run how it normally would run. Once you've seen all you need to see, quietly leave. Later, fill the coach in on what you learned and thank him or her.

One final thing: Let practice be practice. Don't make it any bigger or more important than it really is. Usually, it's best not to bring up your child's performance following practice. It's okay to ask kids if they had fun and what they learned. If youngsters want to talk beyond these two points, they will. Don't press children for every little detail. When you're low key and don't make performance at practice a big deal, you're doing your part to help kids be comfortable about making mistakes while learning new skills.

Avoid Conversations about "How Many" or "How Much"

"How many points did you score?"

"How much did you win by?"

"How many aces did you serve?"

"How much did you play?"

Parents commonly ask their kids these questions after games. Often, parents measure their child's performance based on the "stats" he or she gives them. If a child didn't score or play many minutes, parents might be disappointed in their child and even believe he or she failed.

Numbers rarely tell the whole story. They're just a small part of the picture. Let's take the example of a child who didn't have a hit in four at-bats during her softball game. If this is the only factor her parents use to gauge success, then the child performed poorly. But when other factors are taken into consideration, the picture changes considerably. Let's say she faced a really good pitcher, hit three hard groundballs to advance base runners, and laid down a perfect sacrifice bunt to move another runner into scoring position. She displayed great effort in the field and didn't make any errors. When you look at "non-number" factors like these, this child had a tremendous game.

This is a typical example of how many young players perform. Most kids will try their best but will rarely score the most points, play the entire game, or have the game-winning score. Instead, coaches ask them to give their best effort and play the role assigned to them that best helps the team. These contributions can't always be measured in numbers.

When you stress statistics as the only yardstick for success, kids will too. This promotes individualism and selfishness, both of which run counter to the team concept coaches are trying to build and teach to players. There is nothing worse than a player (or his or her parent) rushing to the scorer's table or grabbing the scorebook first thing after a game to check on how many points the player scored. A valuable life lesson youngsters can learn in youth sports is that, often, people must negotiate, sacrifice, adjust, and change their wants and desires in order to help the team grow and be successful. This lesson helps young people learn how to work well with others in group situations that they'll be a part of in family, school, or work settings outside of athletics.

Instead of stressing numbers and statistics, parents should focus on effort, teamwork, and enjoyment. After a game or practice, your first question should be *"Did you have fun?"* Let kids know that this is just as important to you as it is to them. Also, praise kids for high energy and good effort. Even if they didn't score or only played a few minutes, tell them you are proud that they tried hard and gave their best. Finally, talk to your child about the importance of cooperation and working well with others. Emphasize that individual accomplishments always have to be within the framework of the team's goals. That means, team first, "me" second.

Don't Draw Comparisons between Your Child and Other Kids

Unless it's a compliment, no one likes being compared to another person. Think about how you would feel if your boss openly matched you up against a co-worker on matters like education history, salary record, or job performance. Most adults would be upset and view this as unfair, as well they should. Kids don't feel any differently when their parents compare them to other players in youth sports.

After games, some parents say things like, *"How come you don't pass like Johnny?"*; *"Maggie really hustles; why can't you play like her?"*; or *"You need to get fired up about winning like Javon."* These kinds of statements do more harm than good. They don't include any specific feedback or instructions on how to improve, so kids get confused about what to do. And, when you sing the praises of other players while telling your child he or she isn't quite up to snuff, your child is likely to get discouraged and upset.

Some players will never be able to do what other players can do. All kids are unique (physically, mentally, emotionally, etc.) and have individual strengths and weaknesses. This may mean a child is not the most physically gifted player, but is a good team member who contributes by filling a specific role well. The last thing you want to do is force kids into trying to do things they can't do or into being someone they're not. So, treat each child individually by looking for the good things he or she does and building on them.

When you talk with your child about sports and the team, it's best to leave other players and how they perform out of the conversation. Focus on what your child does well or correctly and praise him or her for it. Be realistic about your child's strengths and limits. The goal should be to help children reach their own potential, which will be unique and different from that of other kids. Always encourage your child to do his or her best, and make it clear that will always be enough for you.

Praise Kids for Their Efforts Immediately after Contests, Win or Lose

Following games and matches, emotions are usually running high. Coaches, players, and parents can be fired up and happy after a win or dejected and disappointed after a loss. Either way, it's not a good time for parents to rehash their kids' or the team's performance. This can be hard for many parents because their first instinct is to replay everything that happened while it's fresh in their minds. Unfortunately, the discussion usually leads to and becomes focused on who (players and team) did poorly and what they could have done better or differently.

Right after a game, parents may not be in the right frame of mind to be objective and supportive, and kids aren't ready to listen. The best thing parents can do following games is just to focus on praising participation and effort, whether it's a win or a loss. Youngsters know the final score and have a pretty good idea of how they played and the effort they gave. They don't need someone breaking down their performance and analyzing it the minute the game's over. Remember, your job is to be a cheerleader, someone who's positive, encouraging, and supportive. Leave it to the coaches to discuss at the next practice your child's performance and the team's win-loss record.

There will be times when games are complete disasters, where your child and the team play poorly and give poor effort. That's when it's best to use empathy. It's difficult and awkward to praise kids when they know they didn't play well, and such comments can come across as phony and insincere. Instead, say something like, "Forget this one. You'll get 'em next time" or "Keep your head up. You'll do better next game." This helps kids stay positive and keeps you from saying something negative in the heat of the moment that you might regret.

Parents play a big role in helping children keep youth sports in the proper perspective. But first they have to examine their own expectations about winning and their child's performance. If parents' expectations and goals are out of sync with their child's, then it's important for them to make some changes. Remember, this is your child's youth sports experience, not yours. You can keep youth sports in the proper perspective by choosing to make practices a "parent-free zone" as much as possible, not talking about "how much" or "how many," resisting the urge to compare your child to other kids, and praising your child and all of his or her teammates for their efforts following every game. Changing the mindset of your youth sports setting may be difficult, but you can take the lead by emphasizing and cheering for participation, effort, improvement, and enjoyment over winning.

PROBLEM-SOLVE ISSUES YOUR CHILD HAS WITH COACHES

There may be times as your child plays sports that he or she and the coaches don't see eye to eye. Problems might involve scheduling conflicts, how a coach disciplines players, missing practices or games, playing time, playing a particular position, strategy questions or clarifications, peer problems, personal issues, or how the coach treats the players. It's not the end of the world when disagreements come up. They're a normal part of life, and provide an opportunity for parents to teach their kids the important and valuable life skill of problem solving.

When youngsters experience something unpleasant or difficult, many parents' first reaction is to jump in to protect their kids and come to their aid. This is understandable; after all, parents love their children and don't enjoy seeing them struggle. But, for young people to grow and learn, it often is best for parents to step back and gently guide their kids through the experience rather than trying to fix everything for them.

Youth sports are actually a safe training ground for kids to practice problem-solving skills. There are caring adults (parents and coaches) who can help steer youth in the right direction so they can experience success.

Youngsters can then take what they've learned and apply it to other areas of life (family, friends, school, etc.) where problems can be a bit more complicated and harder to solve.

The goal of problem solving is to arrive at a "win-win" solution – or as close to one as possible. This doesn't always mean everyone gets exactly what he or she wants. Most times, negotiation and compromise are necessary to get things done to everybody's satisfaction. The following tips for success are things parents can do to help their kids learn how to be effective and successful problem-solvers with their coaches.

Stay Neutral and Avoid Making Negative Comments about the Coach

When girls and boys have a problem or conflict with their coaches, it's sometimes hard for the youth to see much beyond their own side of the issue. They may not be mature or skilled enough to consider the coach's point of view. So it can be difficult for kids to work together with their coaches to arrive at constructive and acceptable solutions. That's when parents need to step in, teach, and guide children on how to solve problems the right way.

Your teaching begins when your child comes to you for help, or when you realize your child needs help. How you first react to the problem sets the tone. If the goal is to teach your youngster to react and behave in a calm, rational, and open-minded manner, it's important for you not to make snap judgments, jump to conclusions, and side with your child before you know all the facts. In other words, be impartial and stay calm and collected from start to finish.

When concerns do arise, don't start the problem-solving process by making negative comments about the coaches. If you put down the coach, your child will do the same. Worse, you've automatically sided with your child and implied that he or she is right. So, if your son or daughter comes to you with an issue about playing time, don't say something like, *"Your coach doesn't know what she's doing. You should be playing the entire game!"* Instead, say, *"There's probably a good explanation for why your playing time has dropped. Let's go over how you can talk to your coach about your concern."* Beginning your conversation in a composed and neutral way helps put your child into the right frame of mind to see both sides of the issue so he or she can go about dealing with the situation fairly.

Practice with Your Child How to Advocate for Himself or Herself with the Coach

Preparation is the key to success in many aspects of life – and that includes resolving conflicts with others. It's especially important for young people who are new to problem solving. The first place you can begin preparing your child is by helping him or her to understand the problem. To do that, have your child clearly and specifically describe the problem situation. Often, kids completely miss what's actually happening and are upset or worried about the wrong thing. Ask some open-ended questions so your child can describe all that he or she thinks is going on. Once you feel you and your child have an accurate read on the situation, ask your child to come up with options (no more than three) – things he or she could say and do – that might help solve the problem with the coach. The next step is having your child write down the advantages and disadvantages of using each option.

Once all this is done to your satisfaction, help your child choose the option he or she thinks will work best to solve the problem and make a plan for how to use it.

An easy way to remember this process is to take the first letters of each main step and put them together. They spell **POP – Problem, Options, Plan**.

Preparation also includes practice. By this we mean role-playing or acting out the situation. You can pretend to be the coach while your child demonstrates the option he or she chose. As you practice, praise your child for the things he or she does well and provide tips and suggestions for things your child could do better or differently.

When your child is ready and set up for success, he or she can ask to meet with the coach to discuss the issue. Depending on your child's age and maturity level and the nature of the problem, you might come along to support and guide your child through the process. If you do, let your child do most of the talking and step in only when needed. Remember, this is an important skill for your child to learn, practice, and use, so allow him or her to take charge as much as possible.

Let's take a look at an example of how the POP method can be used.

Problem

In the last three volleyball matches, Jenny's playing time has decreased. Jenny tells her parents she has gone from playing in every game to playing in just one. Jenny is upset because she doesn't know what she did wrong or what she can do to earn more playing time back. Jenny says the coach never told her that he planned on giving her less playing time, and he hasn't told her why she isn't playing as much. Here's what Jenny and her parents come up with as her options:

Options

1. Say nothing to the coach and just keep plugging away.

Advantages: She could earn back more playing time without having to bother the coach.

Disadvantages: She might work on the wrong things and continue to get less playing time.

2. Talk to the coach about why her playing time has dropped and ask what she can do to get more time back.

Advantages: Jenny would know what to work on, could improve on her weaknesses, and might play more.

Disadvantages: The coach might see her as a complainer and play her even less.

Plan

Jenny decides to talk with the coach about why her playing time has decreased and what she can do to earn back more time. After talking with her parents, Jenny realized that her coach probably won't penalize her for asking him about the issue, as long as she does it calmly and positively. Jenny and her parents then role-play the situation before she goes to the coach.

Support the Coaches' Right to Make Decisions

Your child might do an outstanding job of working through the problem-solving process, practicing with you, and talking to the coach about the issue. But that doesn't guarantee you and your child will get the out-come you're both looking for. Coaches have the final say on almost all issues involving players and the team. They are the authority figures in the youth sports world, just like parents are at home, teachers are at school, and bosses are at work.

We all deal with authority figures who make deci-sions we don't agree with. Many times, we have to live with the outcome, like it or not. This is true for many adults in their jobs. For kids, this might involve having a weekend curfew at home, an assignment at school, or a playing time rule on their team. When coaches make tough calls, the best thing parents can do is support the coaches by accepting their decisions. This helps kids learn to respect a coach's authority and understand who's in charge on the fields and courts.

Supporting your coaches doesn't mean always agreeing with their decisions. It does mean that you understand they make the final call, and that you're will-ing to go along with whatever they decide without hard feelings. This is a great way to model for your child that he or she isn't always in control, and that respecting and accepting decisions made by those in authority is usually the best solution.

Youth sports are a great place for kids to start learn-ing how to solve problems with authority figures and others. When your child has an issue or concern with a coach, you can help by staying calm and objective, and not making negative comments about the coach. Next, ask your child to clearly define the problem, come up with options on how to solve it, write down advantages and disadvantages for each option, and come up with a plan that he or she thinks will work. Finally, respect and accept the coach's decision, even if it's not what you and your child want. Working through problems in this way gives your child a good foundation for being a successful problem-solver in other areas of life.

Summary

Parents have a tremendous influence on the youth sports environment and the type of experience kids, coaches, and others have. When parents' expectations are unrealistic and winning and being the best are overly valued and overemphasized, youth sports can become a tense and negative place. You can avoid this and get on the right path by adjusting your expectations and goals to match your child's. This means, first and foremost, emphasizing enjoyment and fun over winning and being number one.

This chapter discussed seven skills that every parent should master and use in the youth sports setting. These skills – the things to do and ways to act – can help you set and maintain the right priorities. When you have your child get to practices, meetings, and games on time with the right equipment, support the coaches, voice concerns appropriately, praise and compliment rather than criticize, model appropriate behavior at athletic contests, emphasize effort and enjoyment over winning, and help your child solve problems with coaches in a positive way, you do your part to help create a fun, healthy, and successful sports experience for kids and adults.

Playing with Character

Lots of parents and coaches are frustrated and fed up with the way many players act in youth sports today. At practices and games, there are kids who arrive late and unprepared, don't listen to the coaches' instructions or accept their coaching, can't or won't get along with their teammates, trash-talk, cheat, brag when they win, refuse to shake hands when they lose, mistreat facilities and team equipment, and give up when the going gets too tough. It doesn't have to be like this! Your players, your team, and your youth sports organization or club team can be different. You – parents and coaches – can prevent this kind of negative behavior and, instead, teach positive behavior to build and maintain an athletic setting that promotes respect, good character, and sportsmanship, effective teaching and learning, and fun.

Making this happen won't be painless; change never is. But it is much easier to do when parents and coaches work together as a team, supporting and encouraging each other. The *Competing with Character* skills for coaches and parents are a great place to start. They'll help you set the tone for positive behavior and provide the foundation needed for creating the right kind of athletic environment. But there's one final building block to put in place: teaching character-building skills to players. To make this all work, everyone – coaches, parents, and players – need to be on the same page and willing to do their part. For kids, that means learning and using the ten *Competing with Character* player skills.

SKILLS FOR PLAYERS AND TIPS FOR SUCCESS

1. Listen to Your Coaches

- Stop what you are doing.
- Look at the coach.
- Make an effort to concentrate.

2. Follow Coaches' Instructions

- Listen to your coach the entire time he or she is giving instructions.
- Do what your coach says immediately and with energy.
- If you don't understand, raise your hand and ask questions.

3. Accept Coaching

- Understand that coaching makes you better.
- Follow the coaches' instructions without hesitation or talking back.
- If you feel frustrated, visit with the coach at an appropriate time.

4. Get Along with Your Teammates

- Make positive comments to teammates; avoid negative comments.
- Ignore irritating behaviors; don't escalate a situation.
- Remember that everyone is here for a common goal.

5. Have High Energy

- Do everything to the best of your ability.
- Hustle, don't walk.
- Stay on task and avoid horseplay with teammates.

6. Respect Your Opponents

- Don't trash talk or make rude gestures.
- Play within the rules.
- Ignore unsportsmanlike behavior from your opponent.

7. Be Prepared for Practices and Games

- Be on time.
- Pack equipment ahead of time.
- Double-check before leaving.

8. Win with Class and Lose with Dignity

- Congratulate your opponents, win or lose.
- Don't brag or boast when winning; don't criticize or make excuses when losing.
- Take a lesson from both winning and losing.

9. Handle Disappointment and Adversity Appropriately

- Avoid negative physical and verbal displays.
- Learn from the situation.
- Work harder.

10. Respect Facilities and Equipment

- Use facilities and equipment the way they are intended to be used.
- Pick up after yourself and teammates.
- Report any damage to the coach.

In this chapter, we'll introduce, explain, and discuss these *Competing with Character* player skills and their tips for success. Once you understand how they work and why they're so important, it will be your task to teach them to your kids – coaches in practices and games and parents at home and in other places outside sports. A team approach leads to much better learning outcomes. Youngsters won't embrace this kind of instruction without your encouragement and reinforcement. Like all other things in life, they need direction and guidance from caring adults to help them learn how to use skills correctly. The teaching methods you learned in Chapter 3 – teaching proactively, using praise, and correcting misbehavior – allow you to do just that.

This chapter starts with the basic player skills and then moves into ones that are a bit more advanced. We suggest teaching the basics first because it gives kids a good foundation for the skills that come later.

With every skill, youngsters should learn and use the tips for success – the behaviors that make up the skill – in the sequence they are presented. These tips are ordered in a logical way, and using them in the proper order makes them most effective.

While we encourage both coaches and parents to teach and reinforce all these skills, we've worded this chapter to speak primarily to coaches. Our hope is that coaches will introduce these skills to youngsters they are coaching, and that parents will teach and reinforce the skills at home. Most of the time, the words "you" or "your" will refer to a coach; sometimes they will collectively mean coaches and parents. Also, most of the examples for how kids use the skills are related to the youth sports environment.

We strongly encourage parents to read this section so they understand what we are asking youth sports coaches to teach their children and how these skills can be beneficial to kids at home, in school, and almost everywhere outside the sports setting.

All the player skills are simple, user-friendly, and have a lot of common sense to them. This helps make your job a bit easier. Your commitment to teaching these skills to youngsters, holding them accountable for using them correctly, and modeling positive behavior are what will make the difference and help you create an organization and team you can be proud of.

LISTEN TO YOUR COACHES

This is the most basic player skill, and one coaches and parents should teach right away. It lays the foundation for successfully learning all the other skills. Being a good listener and paying attention are keys to success in many areas of life – home, school, athletics, and work. Any adult who works with kids won't get much accomplished with a group of poor listeners who don't pay attention. This is true in youth sports because there's so much to do and learn in practices and games. So, at your first practice, make this the first skill you teach to players. Parents can do their part by teaching and reinforcing this skill at home.

Stop What You Are Doing

This first listening behavior helps kids eliminate distractions. To be a good listener and successful learner, young people need to give their full attention to the person who's talking and giving instructions. This is true at practices, games, home, and school. So, before you begin telling players what to do and how to do it, ask them to stop what they're doing. You might say something like, *"Everyone, I need your attention."* This reminds girls and boys it's time to settle down and begin listening and learning.

Look at the Coach

This behavior helps kids focus their attention on you and your words. Many times, youngsters stop what they're doing but still aren't ready to listen because they're focused on someone or something else. Having kids lock their eyes on you helps them concentrate on your message. You can help remind kids to do this by saying something like, *"Okay everyone, all eyes on me."*

Make an Effort to Concentrate

This final listening behavior is important for players to do whenever you're teaching and coaching. You have information to pass on to players that will help them improve and succeed as individuals and as a team. So, it's important for them to focus on what you say or do. You can help kids do this by saying, *"Are there any questions?"* Or, you can ask a player to repeat what you just said. When your kids know you will be testing their ability to concentrate, they'll make a better effort to really listen to what you have to say.

This skill is simple and straightforward, but it's extremely important. With good listening skills, kids become better learners and you become a more effective coach. So, when it's time to listen, make sure players stop what they're doing, look at you, and make an effort to concentrate. When kids use these listening behaviors, they have a much better chance of being successful in athletics, at home, and at school.

SKILL

Follow Coaches' Instructions

Following instructions is probably the single most important skill you can teach a child, whether you are a coach or a parent. If being able to listen and pay attention is the curveball of skills, following instructions is the fastball. If you're a coach, it's the skill that serves as the foundation for almost every behavior you'll expect from a youngster who's competing for you. As a parent, it's the skill that enables you to guide your child to do tasks around the house, complete schoolwork, and use appropriate behavior (manners, courtesy, showing respect, taking responsibility, and more).

When kids can follow instructions correctly and consistently, they have a key tool that will help them grow and succeed in athletics and many other areas of life. When coaches spend time teaching and reinforcing this skill, practices run more efficiently, kids learn more, and their play improves. In homes where kids follow instructions, there's usually a lot less nagging and fighting, and chores are done on schedule, leaving more time for enjoyable activities. Much of your success and effectiveness as a coach or parent depends on how well your kids learn and can perform this skill, so make it a priority!

Listen to Your Coach the Entire Time He or She Is Giving Instructions

Many kids struggle to pay attention for even short periods of time and often fail to hear and understand all of your coaching and instructions. That's why it's important for you to teach kids to listen to everything you have to say. Whether you're teaching physical or character skills, explaining drills, or introducing game strategy, players need to stop what they're doing, look at you, and concentrate the entire time you're talking. Children need to do the same for their parents when they give instructions about schoolwork, chores, or manners. When young people hear all you have to say, they retain more information, can do what you ask the right way, and become better learners.

Do What Your Coach Says Immediately and with Energy

This behavior is all about action – kids doing what you ask right away and with enthusiasm. For example, if you tell your players at the end of baseball practice to gather the equipment, pick up the practice bases, and clean up the dugout, you should expect every kid to be hustling to get the job done in record time. Sometimes, there's a tendency for kids who don't want to do something to go about it halfheartedly, complaining all the way. By teaching and reinforcing this skill, you gradually help them understand that there may be many things they won't like or want to do, but it doesn't excuse them from doing them with a positive attitude. When you get your players committed to doing what you ask, immediately, and with energy – both individually and as a team – you've helped them take a big step in the learning process.

If You Don't Understand, Raise Your Hand and Ask Questions

No matter how well you explain a skill, drill, or game plan, or how well you think kids are listening and paying attention, there will be youngsters who just don't get it the first time. Even if you see all your players nodding their heads as you explain something, don't assume this means everyone understands what you're saying. Sometimes, youngsters are embarrassed by having to ask a question in front of everyone when they don't understand something. It's like admitting they're not as "smart" as everyone else. They'd rather be confused than look silly in front of their friends. So, you may not see a lot of girls and boys step forward with questions. That's why you have to encourage questions and make young people feel comfortable about asking them. Instead of waiting for players to speak up, you might say something like, *"This is a new drill, and we've covered a lot. I want to make sure everyone understands what to do. Are there any questions?"* When someone does come forward, praise him or her by saying, *"Great question!"* or *"I'm glad you asked that because other people might be wondering about that, too."* You want to make sure everyone is on the same page and knows exactly what to do.

During practices and games, coaches give players many instructions. For you to be an effective coach and players to be good learners, they must know how to follow instructions. That means listening to everything you have to say, doing what's asked immediately and with high energy, and asking questions when they don't understand. When you teach players to do this well, you've set them and the team up for success both on and off the fields and courts.

Accept Coaching

SKILL

When kids make mistakes and fail, they don't always appreciate being corrected by adults. In fact, some of them take correction and teaching too personally and become defensive and angry. You might even be accused of "getting on them." These kids are tuning out your instruction because they view it as something negative. When this happens, relationships between you and your players break down, and your kids and the team stop improving. "Accepting Coaching" is a skill that helps young people understand that mistakes and failure are normal parts of the learning process in any setting (home, school, athletics, etc.), and that adult instruction is intended to help them grow, improve, and succeed.

Coaching is teaching, and teaching involves helping kids learn new skills, correct areas where they struggle, and strengthen what they already do well. As we've discussed, it's important to spend a majority of your teaching time catching players doing the right things and praising them. But it's just as important to provide youngsters with corrective feedback – telling them what they did wrong and teaching them what to do differently – when they make mistakes.

Feedback and teaching occur at every level of sports. This is especially true in youth sports, where kids are acquiring brand new skills at every practice and game. They inevitably will struggle and do things incorrectly. It takes a lot of time, repetition, and teaching on your part to help young people get it right, improve, and, ultimately, be successful.

Understand that Coaching Makes You Better

Players need to be receptive to your coaching instructions. One way coaches can help make this happen is by talking to players about feedback and teaching and explaining their benefits right from the start. You might proactively teach to your players by saying, *"Guys, we're going to cover a lot of new skills and ways of doing things in practices and games. I don't expect you to know or do everything correctly right away. It takes time, and you're going to make mistakes along the way. When you do, I'll give you some pointers and things to do differently that will help you do the skills correctly or better. Getting instruction from your coaches isn't a bad thing; it's a good thing that helps you to learn and improve."* When you get this all out in the open, kids are more likely to trust you and accept what you're trying to teach them.

Follow the Coaches' Instructions without Hesitation or Talking Back

When you give your players feedback and directions for how to do something differently, they should respond by letting you know they understand what you want or by doing what you ask. Coaches want practices to move along at a good pace so everyone learns what's being taught and has the same opportunities to practice skills. When you have to continually stop practice because players are arguing or resisting your efforts to coach, nothing gets accomplished and no one learns. Coaches are authority figures in youth sports, and players need to learn to trust their knowledge and expertise; that means quickly following instructions without arguing or complaining.

Players usually don't see their own flaws or mistakes. Many times, they've become so used to doing something a certain way (often the wrong way) that it feels strange to do it any other way (including the right way). It takes an experienced, impartial, and knowledgeable observer like a coach to tell kids what they need to change and how to do it. For example, a youth coach might see a player carrying a football in a way that makes him more likely to fumble. If the player has always carried the football this way, he's comfortable with it and doesn't see the need to change. But if the youth is going to become a better player, he needs to learn the correct form. He must listen to, trust, and follow the coach's instructions without hesitation or talking back if he's going to learn to do the skill correctly. Having said that, remember that it's okay for a player to ask questions to clarify what you want and to make sure he or she is doing a skill correctly.

If You Feel Frustrated, Visit with the Coach at an Appropriate Time

Players have lots of new things thrown at them all the time. There are skills and drills to learn and master at practice, game strategies to absorb and execute, and advice shouted from the sideline (by coaches and parents) during play. All this can overwhelm, confuse, and frustrate kids. While these feelings are normal anytime we're faced with learning something new, children have a much harder time handling them.

When players feel overloaded, they must understand that they can talk to you. You also must teach them the proper time and way to do it. There's a right and wrong time for players to approach coaches. Unless it's an emergency, during games or immediately after games is one of the wrong times because coaches are preoccupied and players can be emotional. Teach your players that it's usually best to wait and talk with you before or after practices when everyone is calm and relaxed. This way, players can express their feelings and concerns appropriately, and you are better able to give them your full time and attention. Using this approach helps set the stage for a productive and successful exchange between coach and player and a solution that tries to satisfy everyone.

It's sometimes difficult for kids to understand that corrective feedback from adults is a good thing and that it's something they'll have to deal with all their lives. To help young people learn to accept your instructions in a positive way, explain how your constructive criticism and teaching can help make them better, how they need to follow your instructions without hesitation or talking back, and how they can talk with you – at the appropriate time – when they feel frustrated. How well youngsters learn to positively respond to and accept feedback and teaching from adults (coaches, parents, teachers, and bosses) will have a huge impact on how much success they experience both in and outside athletics.

Get Along with Your Teammates

One of the main reasons parents steer their children toward youth sports is so they can learn how to be part of a team. Athletic competition is one of the few settings where kids are exposed to and actively taught how to work together with others in a group. In many other environments, kids are individuals first. In school, for example, even though young people are part of a large student body, the main focus tends to be on individual achievement (grades). In team sports, the focus ideally is on group success and not the individual.

In most cases, youth sports are the first place youngsters learn how to become a good teammate. Knowing how to do this is an important and valuable skill that has relevance in many areas of life, especially in relationships with family and friends, and later on in the workplace.

The first and perhaps most critical step in learning how to be a good team member involves the skill of getting along with others. This isn't always easy for kids (or adults!) to do. A team consists of a group of individuals who are different in many ways. It's unlikely that every youngster will be good pals with all of his or her teammates, either on or off the fields and courts. And there's nothing wrong with that; players don't have to like every person on the team. But they do have to – at the very least – respect and support each other as they work toward a common goal.

In this section, we'll discuss one of the key ways kids can be positive and productive members of a team. When players learn how to get along with their teammates by correctly and consistently using the following tips for success, you'll have a cohesive group that enjoys being together and working toward the common goals of helping each other and the team improve and succeed. There's no doubt that this kind of learning experience can have a profound and positive impact on kids' lives.

Make Positive Comments to Teammates; Avoid Negative Comments

"You stink!" or *"Nice try!"* What would you rather hear from your players after a teammate strikes out or misses an easy goal? Obviously, any good coach would say he or she wants players to say nice and encouraging things to each other, especially when someone makes a mistake, fails, or is struggling.

A big part of your job is to develop and maintain a positive and safe athletic environment where young people can learn, grow, and have fun. One of the best ways to do this is to praise kids for using positive and encouraging language with each other like this: *"Hannah, nice job of getting along with your teammates today. You made lots of positive comments when others did well, and you encouraged them to keep working hard when they didn't do so well. Keep it up! I'm really proud of you!"* This kind of positive attention is rewarding to many youngsters, and makes it clear that you value and expect such behavior from all the players. Finally, it's important for you to model being positive and supportive by consistently and sincerely encouraging your players. This gives kids an even better understanding of what to say, how to say it, and when to say it.

Here's a good example: I had a friend whose son played on a youth baseball team. One day in a close game, a ball was hit hard to right field where the son was playing. He dove for the ball and it hit his glove. But when he hit the ground, the ball popped out. The other team scored two runs and took the lead.

When the inning ended, the right-fielder, who was upset with himself for dropping the ball, was mobbed by his teammates for his great effort in trying to make the catch. When he got to the dugout, he smiled and enjoyed the high-fives. The next time he was at bat, he hit a grand slam home run that ended up winning the game. He was ready to keep playing and trying to help the team because his teammates (and his coaches) had picked him up and helped him forget a bad play.

Some coaches believe that "kids will be kids," and that they're just naturally going to say mean, nasty, and ugly things to each other. While there might be some truth to that, it's no excuse or reason for a coach to ignore negative comments or allow them to happen. Coaches must step up and teach players that this kind of conduct is inappropriate and unacceptable.

Kids don't get involved in athletics to be ridiculed or bullied, and the last thing coaches should want is to create an atmosphere – or allow one to exist – where any youngster is unhappy and miserable. It can be extremely upsetting and damaging to kids when their teammates make fun of or belittle them. That's why all players need to understand and learn that negative comments are out-of-bounds and will result in negative consequences. It's up to coaches to teach this expectation to players and to follow through with consistent teaching and consequences when kids misbehave *and* when they get it right.

Ignore Irritating Behaviors; Don't Escalate a Situation

Almost every group of kids has its share of youngsters who mess around and do and say things that irritate others. This certainly is true for kids on youth sports teams. When this kind of misbehavior happens, it's important to stop it right away and not respond in ways that make the situation worse. Obviously, coaches can do this through remaining calm and teaching, but players also can do their part by choosing to do the right thing.

Youngsters need to understand they can't control another person's behavior; they can only control their own behavior. So, when a youth is faced with irritating and negative behaviors from other players, he or she should only be concerned with and focused on what he or she can say or do. And the best course of action is usually to keep quiet or walk away. When kids choose to do this, they're doing their part to keep inappropriate behavior in check and prevent situations from escalating.

Sometimes, misbehavior from other players might get to be so bothersome that it's hard for kids to stay quiet or walk away. If this happens, they should come to you for help. Once you're aware of what's going on, you can address and resolve the situation so players don't feel compelled to take matters into their own hands.

Also, praise a youngster for asking for your help, and try to keep the issue between you and the youngster. This shows players they can trust you and your ability to take care of any issue, concern, or problem they might have with other kids on the team.

Remember that Everyone Is Here for a Common Goal

Coaches, parents, and kids might think this tip is about winning. It's not. And it's not about trophies, championships, or player statistics. What it is about is why kids play sports in the first place: to have fun, to get fit, to be with and make friends, to learn skills, and to be part of a team. These goals are what players have in common with each other, and whether or not these goals are met determines a positive or negative sports experience.

Off the fields and courts, it's normal for players to have different likes, interests, and personalities. What kids must understand is that the moment they arrive at practices and games, they need to put aside their differences, come together, and do everything they can to help the team and their teammates achieve common goals. First and foremost, this means getting along with other players by respecting and supporting them. When this happens, all players have a better opportunity to achieve and succeed and to have the kind of positive athletic experience they want and deserve.

Teaching kids to get along with teammates is a key ingredient to creating a healthy and positive team where kids have fun and feel comfortable learning new skills. Players can do their part by making positive and encouraging statements to each other, ignoring irritating and negative behaviors, and understanding that all players are there for common goals. How your players interact with and treat each other will make the difference between an enjoyable athletic experience and one that's unpleasant and miserable. So make this skill a high priority on your team!

HAVE HIGH ENERGY

Some kids are good at math or writing, and school comes easily for them. Often, kids are talented at playing an instrument, singing, dancing, or acting. In youth sports, there are girls and boys who are natural athletes; they have the physical tools and just understand how to play a game. Natural athletes are more the exception than the rule, and most of the players you coach will have to develop the physical and mental skills it takes to do well in athletics.

One of your goals as a youth coach is to help all young people reach their potential, whether they're the best or worst athletes on the team. That's where high energy comes in. High energy is simply hustle and enthusiasm. Every player can control these two things; they have nothing to do with natural talent or physical gifts. When kids practice and play with effort and passion, they take a big step toward becoming as good as they can be.

Every coach wants a team full of high-energy players. It makes coaching more fun and makes games and practices exciting and enjoyable for players. Some other benefits include:

- Players with high energy model effort and enthusiasm and demand the same from others. This helps push everyone and the team to improve and succeed.

- High energy lets coaches know kids are interested, eager to learn, and doing their best.

- High energy identifies leaders on a team. Leaders aren't always the most talented players; they're usually the ones who work the hardest and have the best attitudes.

- When players are enthusiastic and give effort, they're more likely to keep playing sports and continue to get better.

This skill is important in many other areas of life, like school, relationships, hobbies, and work. Youngsters who work hard and are committed and dedicated to reaching a goal have a better chance of learning, growing, and succeeding. For kids, especially young children, this skill doesn't come naturally. It has to be taught just like any other skill. Here are the tips for success you can teach your players.

Do Everything to the Best of Your Ability

Coaches and parents can ask nothing more than for players to give their best effort at practices and games. Kids who are willing to do whatever it takes to learn and improve develop a good work ethic, and usually are the ones who do well, both in and outside athletics. It's not always the most talented or gifted people who succeed and achieve their goals. Most times, dedication and hard work trump talent.

In youth sports, youngsters need to understand they can't control a game's outcome. All they can really control is their effort in practices and games. How hard players work as individuals (and as a team) usually determines how well they perform, and the rest simply takes care of itself. Whether it's a win, loss, or draw, coaches, parents, and players should be able to live with the results when a team and its players give it their best shot.

Hustle, Don't Walk

At swimming pools, lifeguards regularly have to tell kids to *"Walk, don't run!"* On most athletic fields and courts, it's the exact opposite. Youth coaches constantly urge their players to *"Run, don't walk!"* Hustle means moving or acting quickly with energy, not standing around waiting for something to happen. Coaches need to know that players are interested, alert, and committed, and the best way players can show this is by hustling.

The way your team and players practice often determines how they will play in games. Here's an example of what hustle looks and sounds like at a girl's softball practice: Every player is busy doing drills or working on softball skills; no one is standing around or waiting for something to do. Girls are sprinting during base-running drills, diving for balls during fielding drills, and running from one station and activity to the next. Also, there are smiles, clapping, and high-fives, and players are shouting encouragement and support to each other.

You must teach kids how to hustle during practices so they can bring those same behaviors and actions to games. This gives your team and players the great energy they need to perform their best.

Now, let's take a look at how hustle and high energy translate from a practice to a game situation. It's the weekly pee-wee boys' football game. Players sprint on and off the field; there's no walking to the huddle or back to the sidelines. Kids are focused on what they have to do and do their best on every play until the whistle blows. They're running hard, diving, and jumping to make plays. The players on the sidelines are off the bench, watching their teammates and cheering them on.

Coaches can reinforce high energy and hustle by catching kids doing the right thing. In practices and games, most kids love to hear a coach tell them, *"Great hustle! Way to go."* It doesn't always matter whether a player makes the great play; what does matter is that a coach recognizes and rewards a great effort. Praise like this is one of the best ways you can reinforce the kind of get-up-and-go you want to see from your players.

Stay on Task and Avoid Horseplay with Teammates

Practice time is limited in youth sports and it often seems like there isn't enough to get everything done. Most youth practices last only about an hour, so coaches have to diligently plan how to use every minute wisely. Kids need to do their part to make practice time productive by staying focused and on task at all times and by avoiding horseplay with teammates.

It's normal for kids to want to have fun and mess around with their friends or peers. But at practices, this behavior is distracting to coaches and players, and interferes with your teaching. Youngsters need to learn to distinguish between when it's okay to goof off and when it's not. Practices (and games), like the classroom, are not the right times or places.

When players are messing around and not doing what they're supposed to do, safety can be a concern. For example, when players horseplay during batting practice, they risk hitting another player with a bat or getting hit with one. Or, when kids aren't paying attention during live tackling, they leave themselves open to hard hits they're not ready for. Obviously, horseplay in these situations can result in serious injury.

Proactively teach players what you expect from them at practice: to be focused and alert at all times and to do what they're supposed to do without messing around. Anything less is unacceptable. You can back this up by teaching and giving consequences when they misbehave and by using praise and rewards when they do what's expected.

High energy involves effort and enthusiasm, two things kids can control. Girls and boys might have lots of natural talent in athletics, school, or music, but in order for them to reach their full potential, they must give their best effort and have a positive mental approach. Often, kids can compensate for a lack of natural ability by working hard and being dedicated. The way players show high energy in youth sports is by doing everything to the best of their ability, hustling, staying on task, and avoiding horseplay with teammates. The best thing about this skill is that when young people learn how to play with high energy, whatever game they're playing will be more fun and they and their team will get better.

RESPECT YOUR OPPONENTS

Participation in sports has nothing to do with "showing up," "dissing," or humiliating an opposing team or player. You wouldn't know that from watching some professional, college, and even high school teams and players compete. Too many of these contests are filled with trash talking, chest thumping, finger pointing, celebratory antics, fighting, and cheating. This bad behavior trickles down to youth sports, where youngsters tend to mimic the athletes they look up to. All this does is create an antagonistic, intensely competitive atmosphere where everyone is so wrapped up in making the other team look bad that no one has any fun.

Athletics should be a place where youngsters begin to learn good sportsmanship and the concepts of respect, courtesy, and fair play. As a coach, therefore, teaching these lessons to players should be one of your top priorities; little else is more important, including winning. Kids need to see what good sportsmanship looks and sounds like, so you must model these behaviors for players and expect and demand that parents and fans do the same.

Coaches need to step up to the plate and say, "Enough is enough!" No more trash talk, rude gestures, or cheating! It's time to emphasize and teach the value of being a good sport. It's time to put respect, courtesy, and fair play at the top of the lineup. When kids can walk away from the time they spend with you with a better understanding of how to apply the "Golden Rule," it's been time well spent!

Don't Trash Talk or Make Rude Gestures

There's an old adage that goes, "If you don't have anything nice to say, don't say anything at all." This applies well here. All children should be able to participate in youth sports and learn without being belittled or harassed by other players. Coaches must teach players that negative, derogatory, and inflammatory remarks or actions toward opposing players, coaches, and fans are inappropriate, unacceptable, and have no place on your team or in youth sports.

Teach this expectation to players and back it up with corrective teaching and negative consequences immediately when misbehavior occurs. This sends a clear message to kids (and parents and fans) that disrespectful behavior isn't allowed or tolerated. Also, teach players how to be respectful to their opponents. For example, you might require your players to clap for opposing players during pre-game player introductions, appropriately acknowledge good plays by both sides during games or matches, and shake their opponents' hands following contests.

Positive behaviors like these go a long way toward creating the kind of team and players you can be proud of. Everyone enjoys playing against good sports. Not only does this make contests fun and respectful, but also reflects well on you and everyone associated with your team, organization, and/or school.

Play within the Rules

When players compete in sports, they agree to play fair and abide by the rules of the game. This code of conduct has existed since the beginning of sport centuries ago. In every sport, multitudes who've gone before us have given their minds, bodies, hearts, and souls to advance the game and make it the best it could be. They worked hard to build a foundation for how the game must be played, and they participated, competed, and conducted themselves with grace, dignity, and honor. When people cheat, they not only shortchange themselves but they tarnish and disgrace the memory and efforts of those people – and the very sport itself.

Players must learn that cheating is never acceptable, and that it carries serious consequences. When young people cheat, they are learning to cut corners and take the easy way to their goals. When it becomes a habit and seeps into other areas of life, they're tempted to always take the shortcut, like lying to their parents to avoid getting in trouble or copying a classmate's homework to get a better grade. Any success accomplished through cheating is dishonest and hollow; it doesn't mean much because it was done the wrong way.

Youth sports are a great place for young people to learn how to achieve their goals the right way. As you coach youngsters in practice and games, teach them the rules of the game and make sure players adhere to them. Also, teach kids the value of hard work and how to improve and succeed with discipline, honesty, and integrity. Instilling these traits and habits in your players, in the long run, is more important than just about any other goal you might achieve.

Ignore Unsportsmanlike Behavior from Your Opponent

"She's holding my jersey!"

"He's calling me names!"

These kinds of statements from players about their opponents sound pretty harmless and insignificant. But kids sometimes move from complaining about their opponents' behavior to doing something about it. They can escalate a minor situation into a shouting match or even a fight. That's why it's critical to teach your players how to react appropriately when opponents get mouthy or don't play by the rules.

Remind youngsters that they can't control what another person says or does, but they can control their own behavior. So, when your players become angry or upset with an opponent's conduct, they simply need to ignore it and walk away. Any other response usually just makes the behavior and situation worse.

Also, teach your players to come to you when an opponent's bad behavior really gets to them. That way, coaches and officials can address the misbehavior and put a stop to it. The last thing you want is for players to take matters into their own hands. It's not always easy to ignore something like trash talk or dirty tactics and walk away, so be sure to give your players lots of praise when they do.

Respecting opponents is one of the skills that sometimes takes kids a while to understand. But once they catch on, they begin to look at sports in a whole different light. When players, coaches, and parents on both sides show respect for each other, they create a positive and healthy environment where kids feel safe and comfortable competing and learning. Your players can do their part by not trash talking or making rude gestures, by playing within the rules, and by ignoring unsportsmanlike behavior from their opponents. Treating others – and the sport – with respect is the right thing to do and something every child, coach, and parent should make a priority in youth sports.

Be Prepared for Practices and Games

Most young people tend to be disorganized and forgetful. It's almost a rite of passage for youth. Before heading off to school or practice, they're usually rushing around at the last minute gathering everything they need. Being prepared is a skill that teaches kids to be organized, responsible, and punctual. In athletics, that means arriving on time (or early) for practices and games with all the necessary equipment. In school, that means being in one's seat before the bell rings and having the right supplies and books. Proper preparation is a key to success in any endeavor; that's why this is such an important skill for kids to know and use correctly.

Teaching this skill requires a partnership among coaches, parents, and players. The coach's role is to organize practice and game information so that players know where to be, what time to be there, and what equipment to bring. Parents are the chauffeurs, double-checking to make sure their kids have everything they need. But players must learn to take on the biggest responsibility. Naturally, younger kids will have to share the responsibilities of getting ready with their parents. But as kids get older, they need to know when it's time to leave the house for a game or practice, be dressed for the activity, and have all their equipment ready to go. When young people can do this, they've taken a big step toward assuming personal responsibility.

Be on Time

Woody Allen, a famous actor and film director, is credited with saying, "Eighty percent of success in life is showing up." Sounds simple and obvious, but it's true! In youth sports, there's a ripple effect when players are late for practices and games. Other players have to wait around, coaches have to adjust practice and game plans, parents have to wait for late practices and games to end, and, in a worst-case scenario, the team might even have to forfeit a contest. When players are punctual, everything runs smoothly and efficiently – practices and games start and end on time.

At school and work, teachers and bosses expect students and workers to be on time. If they're late or absent too many times, students can be suspended or expelled and workers can get fired from their jobs. Being on time is a critical life skill. So, praise your players when they're on time and correct them with teaching and consequences when they're late. This helps kids see that showing up when they're supposed to is an important responsibility to learn.

Pack Equipment Ahead of Time

When players forget their gloves, helmets, kneepads, or any other equipment they need, it creates big headaches at practices and games. Coaches and parents have to scramble and search for equipment to borrow. In some cases (a mouth guard for football), equipment can't be borrowed and a player can't participate in practice or play in a game without that equipment for safety reasons. At best, this can mean having to rework a practice plan at the last minute. At worst, it could mean having to forfeit a game because a child isn't allowed to play without the required equipment. Players need to understand that failing or forgetting to bring all of the right equipment negatively affects everyone, not just him or her.

To make sure they have everything they need, players should organize and pack their equipment ahead of time. It's the same as preparing their backpack the night before school or packing a suitcase before a trip. Players should include the items they're required to wear (hats, uniforms, shoes) and all their gear (helmets, mouth guards, gloves, bats, balls). For some kids, especially younger ones, it's a good idea to have them go through an equipment checklist while they're packing. This helps them remember everything they need, and makes them responsible for getting the job done.

Double-Check before Leaving

Making sure everything is packed and ready to go before leaving is a great habit for kids to develop and use. They can start doing this at an early age in youth sports, and apply it to their academic or other extracurricular activities as they learn what to do. At first, parents should check to make sure children have packed everything they need. As time goes on and youngsters show they know what they're doing, parents can step back and let their kids be the ones in charge of double-checking.

Being prepared is a pretty straightforward and simple skill. But when players can use this skill correctly and consistently in athletics by being on time, packing their equipment ahead of time, and double-checking before they leave, they've learned something that has value in just about every aspect of life.

WIN WITH CLASS AND LOSE WITH DIGNITY

After games and matches, you often hear players from the winning team chanting, *"We're number one! We're number one!"* Following a loss, these same players might be heard complaining, *"We were robbed!"* or *"We should have beat those bums. They got so lucky!"* How your players and fans react to wins and losses and behave after contests reflects the true nature of what your team values and emphasizes. When a team stresses and prizes winning above all else, players and fans will invest too much energy and emotion in the outcome of games. As a result, they get too emotionally high following a win and too emotionally low after a loss. This often results in bad behavior, like bragging and boasting about a victory and complaining and excuse making when a team loses.

The best way to keep wins and losses in the proper perspective is to make sure you're emphasizing the right outcomes for kids. Remember, their goals are to have fun, be with friends, get and stay fit, learn new skills, and be part of a team. Stressing these things keeps players, coaches, parents, and fans focused on the results that really matter, and helps everyone behave like good sports after wins and after losses.

Teach this skill to players in practices and review it again with them (and parents and fans, too) before athletic contests. (It's not a good idea to try to teach this skill on the fly right after games. Emotions are usually running high, and players and fans may have a hard time taking in what you're trying to teach to them.) When your team and fans know ahead of time how to win with class and lose with dignity, you'll have a group you can be proud of and others will admire and try to emulate.

Congratulate Your Opponents, Win or Lose

Shaking hands with opponents after a game is a long-standing tradition in sports. It's a polite gesture that acknowledges the effort and energy opposing coaches and players put into their game preparation, and congratulate a job well done during the game. Also, handshakes are a signal and a reminder for everyone to let go of any hard feelings created during the contest, because, in the end, competition should be friendly and fun.

Teach your players to line up as a team immediately after a game. As they meet each player and coach from the other team, your players should shake hands with each person, make eye contact, smile, and say something like, *"Nice game"* or *"Good job."* If necessary, you can modify this for participants in sports where there is one-on-one competition (tennis, wrestling, golf). This occurs in front of everyone so coaches, parents, fans, and players on both sides will notice any bad behavior, like refusing a handshake, making a rude gesture, or saying something negative. If this happens with one of your players, correct the misbehavior with teaching and consequences right away. Youngsters need to learn to acknowledge the efforts of others with respect and civility.

Don't Brag or Boast When Winning; Don't Criticize or Make Excuses When Losing

In sports, there's nothing more unattractive and unpleasant than poor winners and sore losers. Poor winners brag about their performance and blow their own horn to make themselves look good. They don't care if they bother or upset their opponents, teammates, or coaches. Sore losers complain, criticize, and make excuses for their performance or the outcome. Instead of taking ownership and responsibility for what happened in a game or match, they blame the weather, officials, coaches, teammates, opponents, or just bad luck.

What do good winners and good losers look like? Good winners are respectful, humble, and kind to teammates and opponents. They aren't concerned about building themselves up in the eyes of others. Instead, they praise their opponents' effort, compliment their fine play, and encourage them to continue working hard. These players have a selfless mindset and it shows in what they do and say to others.

Good losers are level-headed, optimistic, and encouraging to their teammates, coaches, and fans. They find the good in the bad and the not-so-good, and they understand it's okay to fail and be disappointed at times. Good losers don't belittle opponents, blame officials, complain about coaching decisions and strategy, or criticize their teammates' play. They understand that you win as a team and lose as a team, and that no one person determines either outcome. Also, they realize that many times after a loss, the best thing they can do is simply tip their caps to their opponents' good play and move on.

These are the traits, behaviors, and actions to teach your players. What youngsters say and do during and after wins and losses is more than a reflection on just them – it's also a reflection on you, the team, parents, and the organization. When young people are humble in victory and help others get back up from a defeat, they've learned something much more important than how to throw for a touchdown or score a goal.

Take a Lesson from Both Winning and Losing

There are many lessons you and your players can learn from wins and from losses. Most of these involve issues of self-control, discipline, and being able to focus on the positive. Often, much more is learned from defeats than from victories. Unfortunately, some coaches and parents focus on the game's outcome as the sole indicator of success or failure, and they miss teaching opportunities that are right in front of them.

What can kids learn from a defeat? They might recognize certain weaknesses that need improvement. They might be motivated to try new and different things, and try harder at practice to improve. This doesn't always happen when a team wins. Everybody feels so good about the result that they don't see the need to change or improve on anything.

Most young people have trouble seeing past a game's outcome. That's why it's up to adults – coaches and parents – to help kids find the lessons and draw up a plan that addresses and corrects flaws and weak spots.

It's always a good idea for coaches and parents to give youngsters some time and space to calm down after a game or competition. This is especially true after losses, when many kids are disappointed, sad, and upset. Let them settle down and gather themselves. That way, players will be in a better frame of mind to listen and fully understand what you're teaching them.

Avoid trying to fix everything right away to make kids feel better. Don't worry; they won't break if they feel bad for a little while. Disappointment and failure, and the feelings they bring on, are inevitable in life and they're certainly part of athletics. Young people need the chance to experience these things and to learn how to deal with them in healthy and constructive ways. A good rule of thumb when it comes kids and losing is that time (and space) is usually the best medicine.

When coaches and parents make winning and losing too important, kids can get overly emotional because they're so invested in the outcome. This often results in bad behaviors and creates players who are poor sports to coaches, officials, parents, fans, opponents, teammates, and the game itself. You can teach young people how win with class and lose with dignity by teaching them to congratulate opponents after wins and losses, not brag or boast when winning or criticize and make excuses when losing, and draw lessons from wins and losses. When kids do these things well, they learn how to appropriately handle success and successfully deal with failure.

HANDLE DISAPPOINTMENT AND ADVERSITY APPROPRIATELY

Kids can experience disappointment and adversity in just about any area of life – home, school, sports, extracurricular activities, and relationships. When adversity happens, kids can follow one of two paths: Run and hide, or meet the challenges head on. Youngsters are much more likely to get through tough times if they face them straight on with courage, support, and the knowledge of how to do it the right way.

Overcoming adversity is the ability to get back up when you get knocked down, whether physically, mentally, emotionally, or spiritually. Adversity and the ability to overcome it are natural and integral parts of sports. There's an ebb and flow to contests and seasons that mirror the ups and downs of life. Setbacks in sports can come in many of the same forms they take on in life: injury, frustration, loss, poor performance, and others.

Participating in sports gives young people the opportunity to learn how to overcome disappointment and adversity in a safe and controlled environment where the outcome, good or bad, isn't crucial in the scheme of life. Youth sports can be a tremendous learning and training ground for teaching lessons about overcoming adversity, lessons kids can apply to other parts of their lives. Girls and boys can take these lessons into the future where the stakes are a bit higher and more meaningful, and where it can be tougher and more important to get through difficult times.

Successfully overcoming obstacles is one of the most important life skills adults can teach youngsters. Without this skill, youngsters are destined to a difficult journey through life, one that can be filled with frustration and failure. This section focuses on how you can teach kids to bounce back.

Avoid Negative Physical and Verbal Displays

It's usually not a matter of "if" adversity will strike but "when." "Sudden change" is the phrase I use with my players to explain adversity. In a football game, an opponent might break a long run for a touchdown or an offense might fumble the football on its own five-yard line. In the classroom, a student who studied hard and prepared well for an algebra test might learn the next day she received a failing grade because of a silly mistake. Or, in the social world, a girlfriend and boyfriend might unexpectedly break up. To successfully deal with these kinds of adverse situations, young people first have to be prepared for sudden change.

Once young people understand that sudden change is inevitable, you can teach them a positive way to respond, before certain situations happen. This preteaching helps kids understand that there are some aspects of a sudden change situation they can control, even if there are many others they can't.

One of the most important things kids can control when facing adversity is their own behavior – how they react and what they say and do. Before athletic contests, stress to your players that they have no control over the officials, fans, and their opponents. There will be plays and officials' calls that go for your team and against your team. Also, there might be bad behavior from fans and opponents that frustrates or upsets your players. Discuss with them how to behave when these things happen – players are to keep quiet, avoid any negative or rude gestures, and stay focused on the game and what they're supposed to do. You can even tell your players to pretend like the officials and fans aren't even there. This helps reinforce the idea that they can't control others or issues that are beyond their own actions and reactions.

Learn from the Situation

Tell your players that disappointment and setbacks are simply "speed bumps" in the road. Everyone hits one at some point or another. Speed bumps might jostle you around a bit and slow you down, but they don't have to keep you from moving forward. There's a saying that sums up this concept very well: "A bend in the road is not the end of the road unless you fail to make the turn." Teach youngsters they will have to make choices and adjustments along the way; it's all part of the journey.

It's important for young people to learn that no matter how bad things seem, over time, they will get better. When I explain this to my players, I use the analogy of having the stomach flu. When it first comes on, you feel pretty lousy and you might temporarily even feel worse. But in the end, you get better and recover. It's the same thing when adversity hits. At first, kids are likely to be anxious and discouraged. They might even want to give up. When this happens (and it will!), encourage youngsters to hang in there, and show your support by helping them work toward a positive outcome.

This comes in handy during situations like being down by twenty points late in a basketball game, seeing the team's best volleyball player get hurt in the middle of a crucial match, or suffering a six-game losing streak. These are times when kids can melt down and want to give up. They need to learn the lesson that they can't stop trying hard or quit just because things aren't going their way. Wins and losses just aren't that important; what is important is that kids learn to stay upbeat and positive and give maximum effort no matter the circumstances.

Keep in mind that problems aren't likely to be resolved as quickly as young people would like. Most youngsters have the mindset, "I want what I want and I want it now." Unfortunately, life just doesn't work that way. Successfully working through adverse situations takes time; most problems aren't solved overnight. That's why it's important to teach players that patience is the key. Patience isn't a quality or skill that many young people possess, so be prepared to help them slow down, not rush or force things, and take their time understanding the lesson to be learned. With most of your players, you'll have to help them untangle the lesson because they'll be too emotional and caught up in the problem to see a logical and positive solution.

Work Harder

In addition to what they say and do in reacting to adversity, there are two more things kids can control: preparation and effort. Some young people are locked into results and get discouraged easily when they don't hit the mark. For example, just about every young athlete thinks his or her team will win every game. Undefeated seasons, however, are very rare. After all, every game has a winning and losing team. So, when your players get upset because they're not winning every game, talk to them about their preparation and effort. If they are preparing as well as possible and giving their best effort in practices and games, let them know the team's record isn't that important. As long as they're doing everything they can do that's in their control, that's all coaches and parents can expect from them.

Knowing how to overcome adversity is one of the most important life skills young people can learn. In youth sports, players use this skill by avoiding negative outward displays (both physical and verbal), learning from the situation, and working harder. Without this skill, youngsters can get lost and spiral into a cycle of disappointment, setback, and failure. Learning how to conquer life's frustrations and challenges enables young people to accomplish great things, even when they face daunting obstacles.

Respect Facilities and Equipment

In the spring (football off-season), I'm an assistant coach for the Boys Town High School track team. Track meets are usually very long sporting events. Many athletes participate and they all try to keep their energy levels high by consuming plenty of foods and liquids. It's safe to say that once a meet is over, a track venue is a pretty messy place with wrappers, drink containers, athletic tape, and other garbage strewn about. That's why, at home and away meets, we have a team tradition: Our athletes pick up the trash, not only in the area they occupied but also in the other teams' areas. And we don't leave until everything has been cleaned up.

A few years ago, as a meet was winding down, I handed out trash bags so our kids could get started on clean-up detail. This particular meet was an important, end-of-the-year event with lots of teams, athletes, and fans, so there was more garbage than usual. Once our kids finished in their area, they moved to the grandstands where the fans had been sitting all day. As we were cleaning up, several parents from other teams came up and told me what a great thing the kids were doing. I explained to them it was all part of teaching our youth how to be good citizens, which is an important part of building good character. They were impressed with our kids and their actions, and commented that their teams and youngsters could benefit from doing the same thing.

A short time later, an announcement came over the public address system from the press box asking teams that had occupied the stadium's infield to pick up their area. Many coaches and athletes heard the announcement but just continued walking out of the stadium. They didn't bother to turn around and honor the request. Our boys immediately hustled down to the infield area and cleaned it up. Later, as we were leaving, the people in the press box came to our bus, thanked the guys, and gave them doughnuts for their effort and thoughtfulness.

Track meets are not the only place where our girls and boys "clean up." It's also a tradition for our players and fans to do the same thing after away football games. At first glance, this might appear to be just a nice gesture. But it's something much more significant in the big picture of helping young people achieve their goals. We believe actions like this teach respect and responsibility, which are vital to teaching kids how to compete with character.

In youth sports, coaches, players, parents, and fans should take pride in their home fields and courts. Volunteers work diligently to care for and maintain the sports grounds (fields, courts, bleachers, snack area, restrooms) and equipment (balls, bats, game gear, uniforms) the teams and players use. Coaches, parents, and players often spend hours each week cleaning up and preparing everything for the next game or match. The right thing for your players (and fans) to do is to treat their own and their opponents' sports grounds and equipment with care, consideration, and respect. They can do that by following these simple but important tips:

- **Use facilities and equipment the way they are intended to be used.**

- **Pick up after yourself and teammates.**

- **Report any damage to the coach.**

Coaches and parents want their players and teams to do well and achieve, but it's important that they go about it the right way. This means learning and putting into practice the skills and traits that embody good character. Having kids do simple tasks like using facilities and equipment how they are intended to be used, picking up trash at home and away games, and reporting any damage to the coach are great opportunities for youngsters to learn about citizenship and respect, two important traits for good character development.

Game Time!

Chris was a member of the wrestling team at Boys Town High School. Ranked number one in the state for Class B at 185 pounds, Chris was an excellent wrestler who had a dynamite season. As he wrestled his way to the finals of the state tournament, his hard work was paying off and he had high hopes of becoming a state champion.

Chris's match in the state finals was close and exciting. With just seconds left in the last period, the score was tied. As the final seconds ticked off the clock, Chris's opponent made a sudden and dramatic move that earned him a point and put Chris behind. Chris tried to rally back, but the buzzer sounded – and the match was over. Chris had lost by a single point in the waning seconds of the most important wrestling match of his life.

What happened next completely astounded and blew away the crowd, local TV announcers covering the state tournament, and others (including myself) who witnessed it. Immediately after the contest ended, Chris smiled, started clapping for his opponent's good move and achievement, and hustled over to give him a congratulatory handshake and hug. The crowd cheered and the TV announcers praised Chris's classy display of sportsmanship. The next day, the newspaper chronicled the event, and the Boys Town Athletic Department was flooded with emails and phone calls complimenting Chris's actions. What could have been a bitter, devastating moment for Chris turned out to be one of his best – all because he chose to compete with character.

Isn't this the kind of positive behavior you'd like to see from your kids in youth sports? Without a doubt!

Unfortunately, this type of shining example of sportsmanship is much more the exception than the rule. Think about it: People were flabbergasted and amazed that Chris would act like such a good sport after losing in such a stunning, disappointing fashion, and his behavior was considered so unusual that the media deemed it newsworthy. What most observers probably expected was for Chris to throw his headgear, kick a chair, grumble, complain, make excuses, or even shed some tears.

Why is it such a stretch to expect players, coaches, parents, and fans to be good sports during athletic contests? There are no easy answers or solutions. But there is a way to start making good sportsmanship and good character the norm in youth sports. *Competing with Character* shows players, coaches, parents, and fans exactly how to go about making sportsmanship and character priorities and "all-the-time" attributes that kids (and adults) can continue to use long after the games are over.

You can help make this happen. When coaches, parents, players, and fans all do their part by using the skills and behaviors discussed in this book, they can fill youth sports with good character, positive sportsmanship, and moving sports moments like Chris's. For this to happen, everyone must compete with character. That means coaches and parents must dedicate themselves to teaching players skills and reinforcing kids for using them, while using their own coaching and parenting skills and modeling positive behavior. Without this kind of dedicated action, the skills, behaviors, and teaching methods presented here are nothing more than good ideas on paper. Your commitment to the *Competing with Character* skills and program will determine the level of success and positive results you have with them.

Okay, game time is fast approaching; it's time for you to step up to the plate! You've learned some new ideas and ways to deal with kids that will dramatically change your youth sports setting for the better. Now the question is: "What are you going to do with all this information?" When you think about it, there's really only one choice: Be bold, daring, and courageous! It's time for you to begin the movement to fix what's broken in youth sports and improve on all the good things out there for kids to enjoy. When you make the change, young people and other adults will follow, too, and before you know it, your youth sports setting can become one that stands as a symbol for all that's good with athletics. In the end, when coaches, players, parents, and fans compete with character, everybody wins!

References

Hedstrom, R., & Gould, D. (2004). **Research in youth sports: Critical issues status.** East Lansing, Michigan: Michigan State University, Institute for the Study of Youth Sports.

Citizenship Through Sports Alliance. (2005). **2005 youth sports national report card.** Kansas City, MO.

CITIZENSHIP THROUGH SPORTS ALLIANCE (CTSA) 2005 YOUTH SPORTS NATIONAL REPORT CARD

The Citizenship Through Sports Alliance (CTSA) is an alliance committed to promoting positive behavior in youth sports by harnessing the collective resources of major U.S. sports organizations to provide practical and proven tools for parents and coaches in youth sports. For list of CSTA members, see page 5.

For the first time ever, CTSA convened a panel of youth sports experts from across the country to evaluate youth sports in the United States and articulate its successes and failures. The panel evaluated only community-based youth sports programs, focusing on those that serve children ages 6 to 14. To do so, panel members relied on their own experiences as youth sports leaders, authors, sociologists, sports psychologists, coaches and parents, as well as on current research and academic literature.

For more details on these grades, please turn the page.

AREA of REVIEW	GRADE
Child-Centered Philosophy	D
Coaching	C
Health and Safety	C+
Officiating	B-
Parental Behavior/Involvement	D

Grading key for each topic:
A = Outstanding; **B** = Good; **C** = Fair; **D** = Poor; **F** = Failing

www.sportsmanship.org

2005 YOUTH SPORTS NATIONAL REPORT CARD AREAS OF REVIEW

Grading key for each topic: **A** = Outstanding; **B** = Good; **C** = Fair; **D** = Poor; **F** = Failing

Grading scale for elements within each topic: **E** = Excellent; **S** = Satisfactory;
N = Needs Improvement; **U** = Unacceptable

CHILD-CENTERED PHILOSOPHY   Overall Grade (A-F): **D**

1. Youth sports leaders, parents and coaches put the goals of children – fun, friends, fitness, participation and skill development – first.
Unacceptable

2. Each player gets adequate attention and sufficient playing time in games and practices to improve skills and promote physical fitness.
Needs Improvement

3. League leaders and coaches reject a "win-at-all-cost" mentality and instead focus on broader issues, such as life lessons and overall character development.
Needs Improvement

4. League leaders, parents and coaches understand the dangers of early sports specialization.
Needs Improvement

5. Youth sports leaders set expectations and hold parents, coaches and themselves accountable for sportsmanship, civility and commitment to a child-centered philosophy.
Unacceptable

COACHING   Overall Grade (A-F): **C-**

1. An adequate pool of coaches possesses training in coaching techniques and safety, ensuring a safe environment for practices and games.   **Needs Improvement**

2. Coaches focus on effort, skill development, positive reinforcement and fun.   **Unacceptable**

3. Coaches cultivate an environment of respect for officials and opponents, modeling sportsmanship and civility.   **Needs Improvement**

4. Coaches ensure that all players receive enough playing time to promote continued participation and physical fitness.   **Needs Improvement**

5. Coaches refrain from encouraging early sports specialization and don't penalize youth who participate in multiple sports or activities.   **Needs Improvement**

OFFICIATING   Overall Grade (A-F): **B-**

1. Officials possess adequate training in officiating techniques, game rules and safety.

Needs Improvement

2. Officials do their part to promote a child-centered philosophy, focusing on effort, skill development, positive reinforcement and fun.

Satisfactory

3. Officials model sportsmanship and civility, encouraging an environment of respect for all.

Satisfactory

4. Officials ensure that games are played by the rules, with special emphasis on fairness and safety.

Satisfactory

5. An adequate pool of trained officials is available for games and tournaments.

Needs Improvement

HEALTH and SAFETY   Overall Grade (A-F): **C+**

1. League leaders, coaches and officials   **Satisfactory**
provide a safe and secure environment
for games and practices.

2. League leaders and coaches promote healthy   **Needs Improvement**
habits – including fitness and good nutrition
– and they discourage the use of performance-
enhancing supplements, alcohol and drugs.

3. The league conducts formal background   **Needs Improvement**
checks on coaches and volunteers.

4. League leaders and coaches emphasize   **Needs Improvement**
the health and safety of the participants,
and they possess adequate training in
first-aid procedures and team safety,
including hydration.

5. League leaders and coaches establish a   **Satisfactory**
reasonable number of games and practices
for each age group to promote participation
and prevent burnout or overuse injuries.

PARENTAL BEHAVIOR/INVOLVEMENT   Overall Grade (A-F): D

1. Parents behave appropriately at games and show respect for officials, coaches and participants.

Unacceptable

2. Parental behavior before, during and after games reflects an understanding of their role as parents and positive supporters – not as unofficial coaches.

Unacceptable

3. Parental expectations are realistic, and parents focus on their child's total development, rather than focusing primarily on their child's potential to earn a sports scholarship or play professionally.

Needs Improvement

4. Parents understand and support children's motivations to play sports – fun, friends, fitness, participation and skill development.

Needs Improvement

5. Parents are willing to volunteer, and they do so without expectations of special privileges for their own children.

Needs Improvement

Competing with Character's ▶
Rules for Spectator Conduct poster (at right)
and skill cards for players, coaches, and parents are
available from the Boys Town Press at 1-800-282-6657
or on the Web at www.boystownpress.org.

COMPETING *With* CHARACTER℠

Rules for Spectator Conduct

- Welcome the opposing team's fans, coaches, and players.

- Cheer *for* your team, not against your opponent.

- Respect all officials, players, and coaches.

- Applaud *all* good plays.

- *Never* use foul language or ridicule participants.

- Respect the facilities and pick up your trash.

- Keep games fun and enjoyable.

BOYS TOWN.

CREDITS:

Book Cover and Layout: Anne Hughes
Front Cover Photography: Mike Buckley
Illustrations: Eli Hernandez